Praise for
Faith Tango

"Carolyn and Craig Williford taught us that it takes *three* to tango: husband, wife, and God."

—LEN and ELIZABETH SWEET, coauthors of the weekly
worship resource www.preachingplus.com

"*Faith Tango* helps you connect at the deepest level. Read it, apply it, and watch your marriage grow."

—DR. GARY and CARRIE OLIVER, coauthors
of *Raising Sons and Loving It!*

"*Faith Tango* will bless any couple that has tried—and failed—to incorporate daily devotions into their frantic married life."

—DA'DRA CRAWFORD, founding member
of the Christian recording group Anointed

"*Faith Tango* frees couples from false assumptions about spiritual formation and provides practical ways to grow in unity and love."

—JILL PHILLIPS and ANDY GULLAHORN, singer-
songwriters and Christian recording artists

"The Willifords buck the tide of tradition to offer a viable approach for spiritual and marital intimacy without creating guilt about 'doing devotions.'"

—MARITA LITTAUER and CHUCK NOON, speakers
and authors of *Love Extravagantly*

"The Willifords encourage couples to grow in the rhythm of their own unique relationships. The authors' insights into relational styles will spark deep conversations and a deeper reliance on God."

—ANDI ASHWORTH, author of *Real Love for Real Life,*
and CHARLIE PEACOCK, record producer and Christian
recording artist

"Finally, an approach to spiritual growth that addresses your hopes and dreams, your passions and joys, even your brokenness and pain. *Faith Tango* frees you to grow together in your shared love for God."

—DAVE and JAN DRAVECKY, authors of *When You Can't Come Back* and *Do Not Lose Heart*

"If you have failed at having successful devotions as a couple, this book will give you hope! Instead of presenting 'ten steps to success,' Carolyn and Craig tell how they moved from awkward attempts at their 'faith tango' to real grace and intimacy."

—DEE and STEVE BRESTIN, authors of *Building Your House on the Lord*

faith tango

faithtango

a liberating approach to spiritual growth *in* marriage

CAROLYN & CRAIG WILLIFORD

WATERBROOK
PRESS

FAITH TANGO

PUBLISHED BY WATERBROOK PRESS

2375 Telstar Drive, Suite 160

Colorado Springs, Colorado 80920

A division of Random House, Inc.

Details in some anecdotes and stories have been changed to protect the identities of the
persons involved.

ISBN 1-57856-562-6

Library of Congress Cataloging-in-Publication Data

Williford, Carolyn.

    Faith tango : a liberating approach to spiritual growth in marriage /
Carolyn and Craig Williford.— 1st ed.

     p. cm.

    ISBN 1-57856-562-6

  1. Spouses—Religious life.   I. Williford, Craig.   II. Title.

  BV4596.M3 W56 2002

  248.8'45—dc21

                               2002006906

Printed in the United States of America

2002—First Edition

10 9 8 7 6 5 4 3 2 1

To our parents
Bob and Freda Wolfe

and

George and Lou Williford
for your examples of loving, committed marriages
of over fifty years each.

o   o   o

We love you!

contents

acknowledgments

This book would not have been possible without the encouragement, prayer support, resources, input, and editing—positive and negative!—from so many. First, we owe our deepest gratitude to Polly for her insight, creativity, wisdom, and constant willingness to read and then read again—at all times and places, and even in response to our last-minute cries for help! *We thank God for you, dear friend.*

We sent out questionnaires to more than fifty couples; those who responded gave us not only the gift of their valuable time but also an incredible resource of vulnerable and honest insights into their successes and struggles with spiritual growth in marriage. *Thank you, friends and family, for sharing your hearts and lives with us—and with all the readers who will benefit from your generous gift.*

Over twenty years ago, we attended a Marriage Encounter weekend. There we learned communication skills that not only changed us profoundly as a couple but also as individuals: how we relate to our children, family, friends, coworkers, those we minister to, and most of all, our God. Therefore, many Marriage Encounter concepts that we use and have adapted to fit our needs are filtered throughout this book. *We sincerely acknowledge and thank that organization for the godly principles that continue to guide our lives to this very day, and if you're an M.E. alum, CYH!*

And finally, our deepest thanks to Ron, Don, Laura, and all our friends at WaterBrook Press who have encouraged, pushed, guided, and prodded us to do whatever was necessary to produce the best book for you, the reader. *Thank you for putting up with us, guys; we love and appreciate you!*

interested in a tango
to a new model?

We began our married life like most newlywed Christian couples: With great determination, we vowed to meet the challenge of growing closer to God in our individual lives and also as a couple. We had visions of spending every evening together poring over God's Word in a way that would move us to ever-deeper spiritual growth. That's what *really spiritual* couples did. Do. Whatever. Thoroughly convinced that we'd share a regular devotional life that we'd cling to faithfully, we plowed ahead with sincere hearts—but also with a good dose of naiveté. All too soon we discovered that the aggressive everyday-ness of life prevented us from practicing the established model that was consciously and subconsciously set in cement long before we said our "I do's."

Now let's stop for a second and ask a crucial question: Who created the assumption that the really connected couples have deep, daily devotions together? Maybe there's an official Marriage Manual somewhere that proclaims: "Couples will study the Bible together every day, ignoring insignificant factors such as whining, arguing, or screaming kids; the inconsequential need for sleep and nourishment; mothers-in-law, school principals, or other emergency personnel at the door; and natural disasters such as earthquakes, tornadoes, hurricanes, and toilets that overflow due to the submersion of a foreign object. They will do this with unrestrained commitment, tremendous energy, and focused attention, finding that their efforts result in an exemplary marriage that exhibits profound spiritual growth. Even in light of the toilet and the mother-in-law."

I (Carolyn) am going to write a new Marriage Manual someday, and mine will feature a unique spiritual growth model that actually fits marriages like yours and mine. (It will also cover the really important stuff like Rules for the Remote.) The old model of a spiritual marriage seems to have been passed down by the generations before us through osmosis. And no one seems to have questioned this assumption despite the fact that few couples are actually able to pull it off.

As you've probably guessed, this assumed model didn't work for us. Period. For years we struggled, feeling guilty and frustrated, failing repeatedly to do what we were convinced we were supposed to do…and what we assumed everyone else was doing. But you know what? We weren't alone in our failure, even though we felt like it at times. Recently we asked a number of couples to share their thoughts and experiences on the challenge of growing spiritually as a couple. How we wished we could've heard years ago what they said about their struggles:

- We try to study the Bible together, but it's rarely successful.
- We failed mainly because we were doing this at night and were just too tired.
- Our lives are too complex and filled with the unplanned to make this work successfully. The harder we try to plan it, the more often something important arises.
- Our failure has been in the consistency department. I talk to God about this… I ask for strength… I ask Him to take control… But then I continue to struggle with it.

And let's not forget the guilt. Guilt is evidently with all of us in abundance:

- Our failure is very frustrating and brings forward a lot of guilt because I basically feel like a loser when I give in to laziness.
- If "the regimen" is interrupted or doesn't come off, then you face guilt; even if it is not genuine, it is still a form of guilt, and that is defeating.

We felt every bit of that as well—the frustration, guilt, and defeat— just the opposite of what a couple's devotional life should elicit. Our friends Karl and Sharon put it in a way that renews hope and desire: "We know we've grown spiritually as a couple by coming through the difficult times—when we had no one else but each other and God. Those struggles taught us the important lessons and drew us together more closely and deeply."

Learning the important lessons. Coming together more closely and deeply.

Those two phrases essentially encompass what spiritual growth in marriage is about: first, what we desire out of this journey together— discovering what's really important in God's eyes—and second, how we want to journey—closely, deeply. Charging right on the heels of those goals, however, is the stark reality of the challenge before us: How on earth do we actually get there? How do we grow spiritually as couples? What really works?

We constantly asked those questions, all the while wading through the blatant evidences of our failure until eventually, something ironic happened. The challenge of finding intimacy with God through our marriage relationship caused us to focus more on the goal—and less on the model. Stumbling and bumbling along, we communicated and sought intimacy with each other. We walked through parks and neigh-borhoods and malls, and we chatted away. We talked in the car, whether we were on vacation, on our way to our new home across the country, or just popping out to the store. We hammered through the issues of life at the kitchen table or in the family room, covering everything from the everyday stuff to the major crises.

The critical point of all this? For some reason, couples have created a false dichotomy. We've segregated all that talking—intimate communication—from the process of growing together spiritually. Something is wrong with that misguided separation—and the resulting conclusion that we're failing miserably in our efforts. For now, hear this one conclusion that you can count on: Growing spiritually as a couple is well within your reach. Don't let go of the goal!

THE CHALLENGE

Rick and Tracy said to us, "What keeps us from doing the activities which help us grow spiritually as a couple? Life gets in the way." Can you relate to that or what? There is indeed an *aggressive* everyday-ness to life that constantly gets in our way! Some days it feels like there's this monster ready to devour you, and it's comprised of appointments, schedules, and a crisis or two thrown in just to keep you on your toes. Forget being worn out by actually doing all that stuff; just a quick glance at your family calendar can hurtle you into a mental break-down—or a glassy-eyed stupor!

No matter who we are, what we do, or where we live, it's still an absolute fact: Life gets in the way.

The Time Crunch: What on Earth Happened to the Month of June?

If you're searching for a word that sums up what life is like in this twenty-first century of split-second computers, instant everything, and impatient, why-wasn't-this-done-yesterday demands, how about this one? *Rush.* Add that need for speed to a multitask, multifaceted life and you have a couple who will find time for what's necessary and urgent—

and skip everything else. As Rick and Tracy added, "There are so many things that are pressing on us every day, and our activities like growing spiritually as a couple just get put on hold."

Job Stress: So How Much Money Is Left in the Checkbook?

What are we feeling on our jobs? Pressure—to succeed, to pay the bills, to keep our heads above warp-speed technological advancements, to prove that we are indeed essential to the companies we work for. The amount of stress all that brings to our relationships is simply enormous. And after a tough day at work, we're supposed to find the energy and desire to read the Bible together?

Children: After Kids, Will We Ever Be Normal Again?

Depending on the ages of your kids (if you have them), you might find the operative word to be *messed...* or possibly, *stressed!* But no matter how young or old your kids are, your life is still affected by a blatant lack of necessities (well, what you thought were necessities before having children), such as sleep, time, money, peace and quiet, and rational thought processes—not necessarily in that order. A friend named Don says it better than we ever could: "When both children were small and at least one member of the family was taking a turn being sick, that was the hardest time to 'be spiritual.' Yet that was when we really needed it. Rebecca and I were running on fumes."

Church Commitments: Did We Really Leave Junior in the Parking Lot?

Sunday school get-togethers, midweek clubs for the kids, Bible studies, youth socials, committee meetings, holiday programs, Vacation Bible School, prayer breakfasts, women's retreats, men's retreats...need we go on? They are all incredibly worthwhile activities, but when do a myriad of activities become more hassle than help? Dare we suggest that too much of a good thing might indeed be too much? Don and Rebecca put it this way: "What hinders us from doing activities to grow spiritually as a couple? Outside demands, work, kids, the phone, even our commitment at church!"

Any of that sound familiar? By now it must be clear that you're not alone. So many of us have been there, feeling the same frustrations and guilt and even defeat. So now—what do we do about it?

THE SOLUTION

We have a suggestion for you, one that will challenge not only your assumptions but also your ability to think outside the box. First, trash all those preconceptions that you have about what devotions as a couple should be. And best of all, pitch all the frustration, guilt, and feelings of defeat with them!

If you're having trouble shifting gears this quickly, then release your previous assumptions and replace them with a totally new model—a solution like no other. In the past, Christians have attempted to practice spiritual growth as a couple in a way that eventually leads to certain defeat because it's inherently flawed in its focus. Our mistake is that we have modeled our couple devotions after the pattern that is designed for individual devotions. One person focusing on God is obviously not the same as when two meet together.

Think of it this way: When I meet God as an individual, I come as one complete sphere. Within that sphere is all of what I am—my thoughts, feelings, desires, and hopes, plus my need of him. And God can indeed meet me there, within that sphere. But when we approach him as couples, we come as two separate spheres. We've expected that, because we are married, we can meet God as though we are already one sphere. What's missing is the process of just how the two overlap in unity—and how that joining then flows toward a shared relationship with God.

In our search for help with this topic, we sent out more than fifty questionnaires to a wide variety of couples. They represent varied evangelical denominations and a wide range of ages, number of years married, and socioeconomic levels. Over and over, they told us, "We've tried the model. It doesn't work." And yet, ironically, from those same couples we also heard, "We have grown spiritually as a couple through everyday life...through crises. We love talking about everything. Being vulnerable and sharing our hurts has been key." Could it be that we've been so loyal to the old model that we've missed the possibilities for tremendous spiritual growth that were right in front of us? Have we been wasting our already-depleted energies on a process that's doomed to failure, when the solution was one we intuitively, albeit blindly, sought all along? What could happen if we combined the correct process with intent and intensity?

That's exactly what we're going to explore in the chapters that follow. We plan to challenge you, guide you, and fill you with hope for a model of spiritual growth in marriage that *does* work. Communicating with intent and intensity, clothed in an atmosphere that's tailor-made for your marriage, just might be the Spirit's pathway for progress as you've never known before. Easy process? Not quite. As a matter of fact, if you think you're going to get "chatting briefly at dinner will do it!" or "Ten Easy Steps to Spiritual Maturity," or "no real change needed," then you're in for a surprise. But will it be worth the effort? Absolutely.

Here's an ironclad guarantee: Give communicating on this level and in this format a fair try. If you're not satisfied, you can have your old relationship back!

Come on this journey with us, will you?

mugs of coffee
on saturday mornings

How Do We Stay Connected When Life Is So Hectic?

t was 1980, and our life was rather interesting. (Isn't it always?) We had two active boys, our very first teeny home with a mammoth mortgage, a budget stretched to the point of snapping, and such incredibly busy lives that we wondered if *we* might snap. Craig was pastoring a church and also studying full-time for his master's degree. I divided my time between mothering and ministering at church. And our boys spent their time being...boys. As in racing cars everywhere, bouncing balls off the ceiling, and drenching our elderly volunteer baby-sitter with the backyard hose. Like I said, life was interesting.

Because we desired to grow in our faith and relationship with God, we still tried hard—despite the busyness of life—to make our devotional life a priority in our schedules. We each had personal devotions, and we also attempted nightly family worship. Before the boys went to bed, we read Bible stories, sang, prayed together on our knees, and sometimes—depending upon how much energy was left at that point—we acted out those Bible stories. By the time we coaxed our guys into bed, we were both exhausted. So now we were supposed to sit down together for a meaningful time of spiritual growth as a couple? Not on your life. All of our attempts to establish a regular time for couple devotions failed because life was simply too hectic.

Can you relate? On Mondays I (Craig) could nearly hear the race announcer yell, "And they're off!" as we charged full-speed into the week ahead. What is it about Mondays anyway? You think you're ready to jump back into the regular schedule, but it's always a bit of a jolt! One day blended right into the next for me as I squeezed in time at my office interspersed with driving to classes; various committee and board meetings in the evenings; study and classwork spliced in wherever there was a spare moment; and time with Carolyn and the boys on my once-a-week day off. Did I mention our spray-painted, held-together-with-duct-tape car? And that I had to patch it back together whenever a piece happened to fall off? Not that I minded. (Carolyn always insisted it was God's way of keeping me humble.)

As for our communication during a typical week, I recall perfunctory conversations on the phone to catch up on the events of the day, attempts to communicate as best we could in the car or during dinner while cleaning up spilled milk or whatever—all the while arbitrating disagreements like, "You gave me more green beans to eat than he has!" Lastly, there were the nights that Carolyn brought up an issue just after we'd climbed into bed and switched off the lights. And she would get mad at me when I only did what I was supposed to do—promptly fall asleep!

I (Carolyn) recall the daily feeling of nearly drowning in motherhood: changing diapers, sorting laundry, refereeing arguments, cleaning up the most recent mess, nursing one or both boys through the disease of the month, teaching by providing a good example, and being constantly responsible for the care of those two precious little boys. I tried to save energy—both emotional and physical—for Craig when he came home, but too many times I was absolutely drained.

My view of our communication was that I felt like a puppy at Craig's feet, begging for some of his time when he came home from work by whining, nagging, pestering, and, yes, confronting him at bedtime with whatever we hadn't had time to solve during the day. Hey, at that point I at least had him trapped in close proximity! And what did he do when I was intent upon in-depth conversation? He snored!

··

Every now and then, you'll find a box like this one. This is a way for us to ask you to stop reading and think for a minute about your relationship with your spouse. Sometimes you may want to use these questions as discussion starters; other times, they might be food for thought for your own personal reflection and exploration. We offer these so that our suggestions and ideas may be adapted to become uniquely yours.

- In the past week/month, have you felt like you are "losing" each other? In what ways, specifically?
- Are there areas or issues that you need to talk about but haven't had the time? Take a moment and list some of the most pressing matters.

··

By the time we got to the weekend, we were both thinking about one thing: recovery. Well, we could hope, couldn't we? Instead, Saturdays were a whirlwind of activities that shoved us right into Sunday—ah, the day of rest!—which included several church services; teaching (for both of us); in-depth conversations with a variety of people; and scheduled and impromptu meetings. After a long day of constant rushing to services and meetings, Craig and I were dead tired, and our little guys were cranky and/or wired. By the time Monday kicked in, we needed relief from the weekend!

Is it any wonder that we began to notice distance slowly growing between us, choking off our intimacy? It was hard work to simply find time for mere snatches of conversation—the type that allowed us to catch up on the basic necessities of the to-do list. As for our hopes, dreams, and deeper feelings, those went unspoken and unshared. There was nothing left over for real communication—not the time, not the emotional reserve, not the physical energy. The only thing we did have was desire; we both missed *us!*

Finally, we sat down and discussed the crisis. We needed time to catch our breath, to look each other directly in the eyes when we were talking, to actually concentrate on a conversation. We recognized that we wanted a block of time to tackle sensitive subjects that threatened to bury the core issues in our relationship with each other and with God. And lastly, we desired the intimacy of sharing feelings that can only come through intentional effort. We recognized that through the craziness of life, we were losing each other. And that was entirely too much to lose.

A LESS-THAN-AUSPICIOUS START

That serious discussion of the crisis we faced in our marriage and the desperate need to have a concentrated block of time to talk led to a brainstorming session. How could we fix this? After listing several ideas, we decided to do something deceptively simple. We committed to talk. On Saturday mornings, for most of the morning. Not impressed? Neither were we, to be honest! We tentatively began this tradition with no pious motivations on our part. In no way did we commit to those Saturday mornings together with the intention that "this would become our marriage devotional time."

As for our goal—other than pure survival, that is!—we focused on in-depth communication at a time in the week when we both had the energy and desire to make it worthwhile. Saturday mornings provided the block of time that we needed and that fit our schedules best. And hopefully, we could limit the interruptions, allowing us the opportunity for amazing, quality, intimacy-building communication. Okay, we admit that we were well-intentioned and naive at the same time.

Our sons were around five and two years of age when we announced with fanfare that "Saturday mornings would now be 'Mommy-Daddy Time!'" Since the family room was in the basement (where we kept the television) and the living room was located off the kitchen on the main floor, we staked out our territory and then quickly ticked off the rules. The boys were to stay out of the living room the entire morning unless an emergency occurred (and infractions had better be real emergencies), certain cartoons were off-limits by Mom and Dad's decree, we would help them get refills as needed, and there would be *no* arguing or fighting between them. (We always threw that rule in, for any event, all the time. Which was a total waste of breath.)

To make this first conversation meaningful, try some starter questions like these:
- **What was the best thing that happened to you this week?**
- **What were your strongest feelings this week, and what event elicited those emotions?**
- **If you could have one major wish fulfilled this week, what would it be and why?**
- **What quality in your life does God appear to be chiseling just now? Can you describe how that's happening?**

Even at those young ages, the boys were a bit skeptical. But they soon warmed to the idea as we armed them with sippy cups of orange juice (you know, those wonderful little inventions that are supposedly spill-proof—whatever) and plastic mugs of dry cereal (also frequently spilled onto the carpet, but fortunately the family dog Hoovered it in no time, which meant that he learned to appreciate Mommy-Daddy Time quite quickly). That very first morning, we enthusiastically began. After sending our sons off to enjoy a morning of silly rabbits and doomed coyotes, we poured our coffee, found comfortable chairs, and settled down for a good talk.

Quite honestly, we don't remember much about that first morning. Were we interrupted by the boys? Several times, undoubtedly. (I, Carolyn, can't recall the details of those early years, but somehow I do have very clear memories of spilled orange juice on the carpet. Our Saturday morning times together lasted far longer than that carpet did!) Obviously, that first conversation failed to leave a lasting impression upon us. But evidently it did encourage us to plan for the next Saturday and then the next.

We were onto something here.

Establishing the Habit

Best intentions aside, we soon discovered that establishing consistency for our new approach would not be easy. We stumbled often, we missed scheduled times together, we messed up by sometimes starting off with an out-of-sorts tone that then colored the entire morning—causing frustration, anger, or hurt—but overall, we did one thing right. We never gave up. Although there were weeks when it felt like we'd gone one step forward and two back, the overall progress in our lives and our relationship remained constant, steady, and encouraging.

Life, however, seemed determined to work against us. The calendar was our greatest competitor and, sometimes, our downright enemy. We battled everything from the kids' activities to church prayer breakfasts to out-of-town trips. No matter what stage or transition we were in, life remained a frantic race. And the main straightaway seemed to be—Saturday mornings.

Then there was the distraction of our responsible, energetic neighbors along with their trimmed-with-a-cuticle-clipper yards. Good grief. Couldn't they just keep their productivity to themselves? In the winter, we'd watch them shovel snow, run errands, and shuttle their kids to all those absolutely essential activities to boost the all-important self-esteem. Arghhh! How dare we make our kids miss even one of those opportunities? We battled guilt every time the neighbors' vans drove by.

When the weather was nice, we could enjoy sitting outside on the porch—while listening to the neighbors mow their grass, weedwack, edge the lawn, all the projects we needed to do in our own yard. And what were we accomplishing in the midst of all that neighborhood activity? Well, we were communicating. But was talking *that* important? Later, when we were slaving away in the yard during the heat of the day, our savvy neighbors were enjoying lemonade on their porches, probably shaking their heads at our procrastination!

Remember also that we began this tradition way back in the dark ages, long before voice mail and even before every home had an answering machine. Often we would be in the middle of an intense discussion when the phone would ring. Was it an emergency? Could it be one of our parents? A church member who was seriously ill? Or was it a telemarketer wanting us to refinance with a lower mortgage rate? Sometimes we just let it go, and sometimes we didn't; sometimes we chose well, sometimes not. Needless to say, we bought an answering machine soon after they became affordable.

There were also mornings when communicating was…umm… difficult at best. Christian psychiatrists and psychologists advise that painful experiences must be shared verbally before a person can find complete healing, but achieving that goal means that you must feel worse before getting better. We know that advice to be absolutely true. It is incredibly painful to resurface and share hurt feelings—and to hear them from each other. After initially being criticized by someone, I

(Carolyn) don't enjoy bringing up that hurt and experiencing the pain yet again. But ultimately, like cleaning infection from a wound, this is indeed a necessary step in our ongoing pursuit of marital intimacy. We find that we must remain focused on the future benefits to find the courage to wade into this area in the first place. The reward is that core issues are exposed, processed, and eventually resolved. Possibly the greatest benefit (and one that we would not recognize nor understand for years) was that we were learning how to be more intimate with our God. Exposing our feelings to him also can be difficult, but as we practiced this skill with each other, we were learning how to share feelings with a loving and accepting God too.

••

What time of the week might work best for you? Can you come up with at least two possibilities to test?

Setting a regular, weekly time to talk is easy, but following through is one of the toughest things you'll ever attempt. So get your battle plan together now: What do you envision inhibiting or interfering with your commitment to talk regularly? List these potential obstacles specifically, and then jot down how you plan to counteract each one.

••

Lastly, some Saturday mornings may have found us simply out of sorts, sifting through frustrating experiences from the week related to work or relationships, exhausted from issues with our kids, or distracted by chores or other responsibilities. Week after week, it was quite clear to us that nothing about life was going to make this commitment to Saturdays easy!

At this point, you may be thinking to yourself, "Oh my. If they're suggesting we stop everything to talk on Saturday mornings—of all times—then that would never work for us!" If so, please hear us clearly:

We're not suggesting that Saturday morning is the only possibility. What we are saying is that you must work hard to find the right time for your relationship. "Your time" might be Tuesday nights, Sunday afternoons, Thursday mornings. Maybe you'll need to test several different days before one stands out as the best fit for you. We're offering you the opportunity to adapt this material for your unique lifestyle and needs. It's up to you to make sure it's a tailor-made fit!

SURPRISED BY PURE PLEASURE, PUZZLED REACTIONS, AND EVEN TOUGH TIMES

Fortunately, amidst the frustrations of distracting phone calls, tense conversations, and watching neighbors get a headstart on weekend chores, we discovered that positive things were indeed happening. And the emerging benefits were encouraging enough to keep us committed. For example, one of the benefits we soon noted was how much we looked forward to our time every week. Strange, but you know how the anticipation of something can be almost as much fun as the actual doing? That's what we still feel nearly every week, and a major contributor to that sense of anticipation is the now nearly ingrained habit of "tucking away" highlights from the week before—humorous happenings, insights from prayer times, stress at work, whatever.

So often I (Carolyn) have thought something like, "Oh, I can't wait to tell Craig about the hilarious e-mail I received, but I'll save it for our time together. That way I can stretch out the story and savor watching him enjoy every moment of it!" Or maybe my thinking goes more like this: "Craig's had such a rough week. Even though I've got to confront him about how much that incident on Thursday hurt me, it can wait until the weekend. We'll wade through all the feelings then, when we're both better able to deal with the emotional work this is going to call for."

I (Craig) have been surprised by how often my emotions are ready to surface by Saturday morning—feelings that I sometimes didn't even know were hidden or buried. When I'm under stress and conflict at the office (and when *isn't* there either stress or conflict at the office?), Carolyn will often press me with questions like, "Didn't that make you angry? Certainly he hurt your feelings! Didn't that bother you at all?" But all she gets at that moment is my shrugging shoulders and nonchalant response. Generally at that moment, I didn't note feeling much of anything.

Because of my background and the person that I am, I have a tendency to delay the actual feeling of my emotions. But as the week goes on and Saturday arrives, I relax in my recliner with a good cup of coffee. As I replay the week with Carolyn, sometimes only then do I realize that I did indeed feel offended or insecure or rejected. Quite honestly, if it weren't for our commitment to that time together, I can't imagine how many pent-up feelings would remain buried within; they'd never surface and be processed, nor would they be shared with my wife, who truly desires to know my heart.

Another totally unexpected benefit we've noted is how our commitment has affected our sons over the years. When they were small— on a purely base level—they obviously enjoyed the uninterrupted time to watch television! But it wasn't long before we saw an interesting trend. Sometimes one or both would forget the drill and wander into the living room where we were talking. After finding out that there was no emergency, we'd remind the offenders that it was our time to talk. Interestingly, they would almost always dramatically roll their eyes, grin, and mischievously announce, "Oh, that's right! It's Mommy-Daddy Time. Well, excuuuse us!" The feigned irritation was merely a smoke screen. Their response was, in every way, evidence that our ritual had become a security blanket of sorts. The fact that we were deeply committed to connecting with each other seemed to give them a lifeline—

especially during those times when some of their friends were suffering through their parents' painful divorces.

••

Can you envision yourselves attempting this strategy? What positive benefits might you experience immediately? What long-range advantages might you enjoy?

••

Even throughout their teenage years, though packaged a bit differently, their reactions were almost exactly the same. They'd gripe about our "hogging the family room" (at this stage, cartoons were definitely out; they were asleep until nearly noon!), making it evident that they found bedrock security in the fact that we were still committed to each other, still talking away on Saturday mornings. We've heard them "brag" to friends (you understand that teenage bragging has to be disguised as disgust somehow) about "how our parents talk all morning," and even warn overnight guests about invading "their"—meaning selfish Mom and Dad—family room. But it was all done in that tone of voice—the one that hints and even insists, "This makes us feel secure. Please don't stop!"

In a similar vein, we wonder if other couples have vicariously benefited from our insistence on our commitment to intentional, weekly times of communication. Church staff members, laity, friends, and family have all heard about our tradition throughout the years, and whether they responded with a "You do what?" type of puzzled reaction or appeared genuinely intrigued, we certainly left some sort of impression! Craig has turned down speaking engagements, passed up golf (yes, women—even golf!), and rescheduled meetings. Men and women clearly noted his commitment to us as a couple, and that spoke volumes about how much our Saturday mornings meant to him.

And lastly, those toughest of times—the days when major confrontations were necessary—were a surprise too. Why? Because when we compare the discussions that pushed us the most, the times of sharing that called for the greatest vulnerability and trust, the Saturdays when we can recall moving closer in our intimacy…we would most definitely point to those tense and painful times. In our individual spiritual growth, we often see the painful lessons as those when we grew the most. Although we certainly don't want to repeat them—nor do we go about looking for more "opportunities" for pain and therefore growth—the fact remains that they do indeed push us to trust God and know him more intimately. Craig and I feel the same way about our confrontational times. We never want to feel that kind of pain again. But we are grateful for the growth that we gained. Once again, God was involved. And he's always about miracles, it seems!

THE DISCOVERY OF SPIRITUAL GROWTH

Over the next several years, we moved from state to state; we weathered the stages, transitions, and changes that life brings; and the day of the week that was "ours" sometimes changed. But two constants remained: a morning committed to us and the ever-present guilt that we still weren't practicing the assumed model for couple devotions.

However, when we were approaching fifteen years of this tradition (we're admittedly rather slow learners in this respect), we discovered something amazing. Our skills at sharing—practiced week after week and bolstered by certain guidelines (more about those in the chapters ahead)—progressed and grew into real intimacy. The more we were able to intimately share with each other, the more that in turn taught us how to be intimate with God in our individual lives. That growth was then reflected in our times together, creating this endless circle of one fueling and feeding the other. We were growing in our individual lives with God due to our Saturday mornings, and our growth as a couple from our weekly intentional communication was also providing incredible spiritual growth for us as individuals. After all those years of feeling guilty about not "doing devotions," we had stumbled onto a process that actually enhanced spiritual growth. Was this the "devotional life" we should have been seeking all along?

We can both remember those initial conversations, the questions, the freeing feeling of beginning to throw off years of guilt. Still stuck in our stubborn ingrained beliefs, we fought the facts before us, argued with the evidence, asked each other, "This can't be, can it? Did all that actually happen just from our commitment to really connect every week?" But there was no denying the truth: We had grown as individuals and as a couple from merely talking. *Merely* talking? Or was there much more to this? It soon became apparent that it was time to break down the process, discover what all it entailed, and, finally, share that with others.

It's been over twenty years, and we're still at it—although now we're in the midst of a mostly peaceful empty nest, a heavy travel schedule, and a still-packed calendar. But as we look back over the years, we both agree that those weekly times of intentional connection have been the single most important investment in our marriage. Never did we envision the depth that would result from merely talking week after week, year after year. Never would we have guessed how tenaciously we would cling to this tradition. And never would we have imagined that both of us would honestly say that the two greatest influences upon our spiritual growth and personal intimacy with God have been our individual devotional lives and our Saturday mornings together.

Wherever you are in your marital journey—newlywed, middle-aged, empty-nest, or coasting through retirement—you can grow in your couple relationship. And whether you've managed to be disciplined in your couple devotional time, have sporadically tried various approaches, or maybe never had any scheduled "formal" time together, you can always begin anew. Today. Try a Friday night date. Set aside undistracted time to talk this weekend. Or maybe you have some free time this Tuesday morning? You just may discover that once you start, you don't want to stop!

. . . .

Balking at that level of commitment? That's understandable, so why not ease into it slowly with these ideas:

- **Plan a "date night" out—for several weeks in a row. Allow that to slowly develop into a regular and intentional time to talk.**
- **Begin with small, manageable blocks of time. Schedule an hour per week, but keep those appointments. Remember to schedule your time together for the best time of the week— the time that will minimize interruptions and maximize your energy level!**
- **Agree to meet for breakfast or lunch, but also agree to pick a topic for discussion ahead of time and stick to your chosen topic. Don't follow the temptation to stray back to the to-do list for the day or week.**

Those of you who are more adventurous by nature may, however, plan to jump right in—starting this weekend!

. . . .

Here is one of the most amazing privileges about growing intimately in our relationship with God, as well as in our marriage: We never "arrive." There are always more journeys ahead, more opportunities, more challenges. This challenge is before you now. We're here to help and guide and provide plenty of suggestions. Most of all, God is readily available to direct—and bless—your journey.

Bought that coffee yet?

do-over!

Is There Really a Guilt-Free Devotional Life for Couples?

(Craig) remember when my friends and I played four-square as boys. While serving, sometimes we'd accidentally send the ball bouncing out of the game area. Many times we insistently demanded at that point, "Do-over! I get a do-over!" It was a simple and quick way to a new start and, hopefully, a better one! That's just what we're going to do now: start fresh, wipe the slate clean, and best of all, seek renewed hope. So let's begin by looking at spiritual growth with a "do-over" in mind; we'll evaluate what it is…and is not.

A number of years ago, I became fascinated by how spiritual growth happens (I prefer the phrase *spiritual formation* to describe this aspect of Christian life). I began to investigate the processes God uses to bring about growth in our lives and how those processes work. The more I studied (eventually choosing to concentrate my doctoral research on the topic), the more difficulty I encountered in striving to describe this awesome transformation. The body of information includes numerous approaches and categories that attempt to describe what spiritual formation actually is.

Is spiritual formation mystical? Absolutely. But does that mean it can't be looked at systematically for patterns and stages to help all of us grow spiritually? Definitely not! I also believe our God has a unique journey designed for each believer. Therefore, at the same time that we try to find similarities in the tasks, stages, and transitions that contribute to spiritual formation, we hit up against the very creative originality of not just each spiritual journey, but the individual believers themselves!

••

Can you recall a time when you grew spiritually through a crisis? Think also about times you grew spiritually through a small group of Christian friends who encouraged you during a difficult period. Or have you grown as a result of methodically following a routine of Bible study and prayer? Share one of these episodes with your spouse, helping him or her to experience the depth of that situation with you.

••

At the risk of oversimplification, however, let me at least attempt to define what I mean by spiritual growth in this context: *Spiritual formation is the process of becoming more like Christ in what we think, what we value, and how we act.* The points that follow further illustrate how this process unfolds:

- Among other things, the Holy Spirit uses the Word, prayer, and the stages and crises of life to conform the believer to the person God desires him or her to be.
- We grow in our relationship with God, coming to know him more intimately.
- Though sometimes mystical and indescribable, spiritual formation can also be methodical and merely a matter of obedience, as in choosing to regularly submit to those who exercise authority over us.
- It is miraculous, hard work and incredibly rewarding— sometimes all at the same moment!

The Process of Transformation

Just as we encounter challenges in defining individual spiritual growth, we move into even more difficult territory as we try to define spiritual formation as a couple. Unfortunately—as we've already discussed—we come to this with plenty of assumptions, baggage, and guilt. So before we begin defining this process, let's first focus on unloading all of those.

Growing spiritually as a couple is *not...*

- becoming a picture-perfect pair who never argue, disagree, or confront each other.
- experiencing gooey, touchy-feely, and "we're-so-in-love" feelings all the time.
- expecting those same responses—the gooey closeness and lack of struggle—in your shared relationship with God.
- limited to the two of you sitting down with an open Bible between you, digging deeply into a certain passage.
- always wading through the mystical and indescribable, although sometimes this might be the case.

The real heart of spiritual formation for couples is a deep relationship with God that transforms our very lives together. While we often think of transformation as a dramatic change, in reality it is a lifelong journey that helps us conform to Christ's image.

Growing spiritually as a couple *is...*

A Transformation for Three

As couples, this perspective reflects our belief that we are not just two individuals struggling through life together, but that we have the company of God as the third part of a "triangle" we created when we entered the covenant relationship of marriage. Peter and Molly see their conforming to Christlikeness as "realizing most that God is the center of our lives and we have the same goal and purpose. That unifies us and makes us stronger spiritually, since we feel so dependent on God then."

A Transformation That Needs Encouragement

Transformation takes place when I encourage and help my spouse fully develop into the person God created him or her to be. That is then reflected in our strength as two individuals who have become one in marriage.

Daryl puts this into actual practice with his wife, Kim: "I ask about her personal times with God. I encourage her to pray for her own struggles and fears." And Robin appreciates her husband, Dave, because "he believes in me as a person, and this has given me the confidence to grow in my own personal relationship with God."

Several people had affirmed that I (Carolyn) had the gift of teaching, but I still inwardly doubted the level of those abilities. Then I heard Craig praise my skills in front of a class—insisting that he knew they'd always rather hear me teach than him—and my heart surged with joy. With that kind of public praise from Craig, my confidence soared! What a gift he had given to help release my gift.

A Transformation That Is Sometimes Mysterious

Spiritual growth can be mystical and indescribable, wonderfully emotional and loving. Pam's vulnerable description of her and Dwayne's crisis of relationship and healing is incredibly touching: "Even now, if I find my mind wandering during a worship service or if my worship lacks freshness in my heart, I need only to mentally return to that awful, miraculous year. I can slip my arm through my husband's and close my eyes as we sing, and I'm transported back to remembering the awesome healing God has done in our lives and in our marriage. And again the tears of thankfulness come."

A Transformation That Is Also Sometimes Practical

The process of moving toward Christlikeness can be pragmatic and down to earth, to the point of confrontation, discussion and/or argument, forgiveness, and healing between you and your spouse. John and Laura freely admit, "We've grown spiritually as a couple when one of us hurts the other. Confession and prayer do wonders in drawing us closer to God and each other."

When Carolyn confronts me, I (Craig) generally react with defensiveness—which is merely a cover for hurt. But when we work hard to discover the core issues and get beyond the barrier that has come between us, we're even closer than before. That's God's grace in action.

A Transformation That Happens
Through Daily Life

Transformation flows from and hits up against the daily-ness of life—its inherent transitions, stages, crises, processes, and demands for change. The couples we surveyed, of all ages and stages of life, saw this happen repeatedly.

From a young couple: "We've had some really good conversations on the way to Wal-Mart!" From a middle-aged couple: "Our best times of growth and mutual encouragement come through the everyday issues of life." And finally, from a couple married more than forty years: "We feel we grow together in the normal, uneventful happenings of life too; we feel this also is God's plan."

A Transformation That Can Hurt

Being transformed by God can indeed be painful—felt deeply through crisis—as Randy and Serena attest: "We only had each other and the Lord; we had to leave to him what we couldn't possibly handle. That act increased trust because it was beyond our capabilities."

A Transformation That Requires Trust

Real growth can only happen when a relationship involves intimacy, vulnerability, and trust levels that reveal the depth of our individual relationships with God. My intimacy with God mirrors and parallels my intimacy with my spouse; my intimacy with my spouse mirrors and parallels my intimacy with God.

....

Can you think of a recent time when the two of you grew spiritually? What were the circumstances that compelled you to grow? Share and compare your experiences with each other.

....

Daryl reflects on this principle: "I find that if my walk with the Lord is where it should be, Kim's walk tends to be also. If my walk is faltering, her walk falters too. It seems the bond between us is very strong."

Carolyn and I tend to use this principle as a litmus test for our relationship. We know that when one relationship is not healthy, the other is likely to be "off" in some way too. Keeping track of both—my relationship with God and with Carolyn—alerts me to potential problems and tends to put a guard around each one.

A Transformation That Is Varied

As we said earlier, God designed a unique journey for each of us. While that journey might sometimes take place as a couple studies a passage in the Bible, it can also happen when a couple sits in the family room drinking coffee together, with tears flowing, sharing the hurt and pain of the last week and how it has impacted their concepts of just who their great God is and what he's doing in their lives.

Dwayne and Pam have experienced that same fulfillment from in-depth communication: "We have meaningful discussion sparked by something virtually every day of our lives, I think. We have never separated our faith conversations from the rest of our lives, so I guess the two flow together a lot. Sometimes the conversation stays lighthearted and even silly; sometimes it's just a list of the day's events. But other times it leads into conversation that both of us grow from."

GIVING AWAY DOESN'T RESULT IN HAVING LESS

As we read what these couples have shared, isn't it phenomenal that neither spouse lessens in personhood or value if the bond grows in the way God intended? Some who deny the worth of marriage in today's society would have us believe that one person must lose an independent sense of self in marriage, thus elevating one partner to the other's detriment.

However, I find it nearly beyond description that, as I (Carolyn) become more fully who God intended me to be through Craig's encouragement, Craig does not become less in our union. Nothing is taken from him as I become more. And as I encourage Craig to become all that God wants him to be, I don't become less in that process either. By giving to each other, we don't lose parts of ourselves (unless we include self-centeredness and loneliness); we don't become less in our personhood. On the contrary, we both just grow in our spiritual formation as individuals and in our marriage. That is amazing.

The couples we interviewed gave numerous testimonies to that aspect of giving: When both spouses are fully committed to the transforming work of God in their lives, they simply cannot give more than they receive from each other or from God. And rather than feeling depleted, they only know more love, more forgiveness, more desire to grow in God for each other. The sum of two people freely loving, supporting, and giving to each other results in each receiving more, not less. It's kind of like taking a numeral to the "nth power," when a number is exponentially multiplied by itself. The depth and power of that are endless!

Tracy says this of Rick: "I feel like I can't give back to him in the ways he has given to me. This has shown me a glimpse of the Lord's provision in my life: He gives without end, and He loves to do it. It is right for me to feel unworthy of His gifts—for I am. On another note, I've learned about God by watching Rick forgive. God has shown me a lot about forgiveness and grace by granting Rick the strength to forgive me." And then, the endless circle goes on, as Rick shares: "Tracy has helped me to understand God's true meaning of love in the fact that it comes so unconditionally from her. That helps me to understand how unconditionally it flows from Him."

We're sure that Ginger speaks for many of us when she confides that she and Trent "went through a very hard time and had to be there for each other when we were down. I watched Trent search and grow and it made me grow too. I had the peace that he needed to find."

There is no sense of one taking and then depleting the other here; there is only a giving and a desire to give in return. Competition is virtually nonexistent too, for couples seeking spiritual growth realize that they're on the same team. And when each is diligently seeking a growing relationship with God, somehow that compounds and multiplies and infuses the other with faith, trust, and strength.

• •

In what ways do you judge that you simply cannot outgive your spouse? How does that model God's love and grace to you? Ponder the question individually, and then share your perceptions with each other as yet another "gift."

• •

At this point, some of you may be struggling with the reality that your spouse is not as eager to grow in his or her relationship with God as you are. You may be thinking, "How can I encourage my spouse in a nonthreatening way? What practical suggestions do you have for me?"

First of all, we suggest that you commit to being a "spiritual sponge" —soaking in not only the Word and prayer times (and obviously, prayer for your spouse) but also Christian radio and songs, books, and any conversations that you can benefit from. Then use any nuggets of truth that you glean as springboards to share in a very natural, conversational way with your spouse. Focus on what encouraged or strengthened you rather than attempt to apply them to your spouse's life. This approach can lead to two results:

- Your spouse will see that you are taking the responsibility for your own spiritual growth, freeing him or her from possible guilt, and
- He or she may also be encouraged or uplifted by what you've shared.

Above all, you should not preach, push, nor in any way expect spiritual results from your spouse. Instead, you need to gently nudge him or her through encouragement. Sharing your week, your feelings, your highs and lows, and what God has shown you personally through the daily-ness of life—again, in a nonthreatening manner—can lead naturally to the next step of greater commitment on your spouse's part.

THE EMPOWERING ROLE OF PRAYER

Another mystical and incredible dynamic in this process is prayer. Most couples told us they wished they prayed together more often, but they definitely went to God in prayer together for anything from everyday issues to crisis times. Even though the couples expressed the ever-present guilt, they also noted incredible benefits from praying together.

Oneness

We're convinced that it's impossible to pray together and not become closer. Peter and Molly said, "We usually pray together when something is weighing heavy on us. It usually restores calm, and we feel more united when we go to God together. Prayer brings a certain oneness that we really don't feel any other time."

Bonding

A great mental picture of bonding may be to envision two objects glued together. When issues of life feel overwhelming, a healthy bonding between husband and wife, as Allen and Eileen demonstrate, can carry us through those times: "Prayer is definitely a key factor in growing close to each other. It allows you to reveal your heart to the Lord. It is an outpouring. It allows you to share the burdens of life with each other."

After a long morning of intense communication, I'll often climb onto Craig's lap as he sits on our oversized recliner, lay my head against his chest, take a deep breath…and rest my worries and fears before God as we seek his direction through prayer together. The bonding that I feel at those times is indescribable. It can only be God-designed.

Relationship

"Praying together is work and, yes, it is positive in the relationship-building process and thus in the spiritual growth process, too," share Karl and Sharon. "It has taught us lessons about ourselves, our failings, and our strengths. This is how we are available to support one another in times of need."

Strength and Support

As Randy and Serena have found, "Prayer strengthens our relationship with each other and with him. We unite our hearts and our minds—which then unites us before him—to share needs, concerns, and joys."

I love hearing Craig pray for me. No other voice on this earth imparts the level of support and strength that Craig's gives, and especially when I realize that he's before the very presence of God. I also love praying for him, simply sharing from my heart his needs, struggles, desires. Like an invisible cord, our prayers for each other build a relationship that is strengthened word by word.

Healing

When there are issues between us that have created a destructive barrier, prayer becomes a powerful tool. Discovering that prayer can help erode those walls, Rick says, "When we're fighting, Tracy is the one to initiate reconciliation. This mostly has to do with the way she processes emotions: When she's angry, she just gets her feelings right out in the open. But I'm more guarded when I'm angry, so I close up more. Praying is a way for us to meet in the middle—and ease tension!" And Dean and Carol agree that "prayer helps you know one another in a different way. It helps resolve conflict by talking to God about the issue and seeing it in perspective."

Vulnerability

Prayer has a way of stripping us; it not only allows vulnerability to happen but also appears to encourage openness. Jamey excitedly shares, "I believe when Ken and I pray together we expose everything to God; it's great to see your spouse humble before the Lord!"

Truthfully, I (Craig) don't like feeling vulnerable. I doubt that it will ever be easy for me to purposefully make myself vulnerable, but real prayer—honest and direct dialogue with God—is a constant goal in my life. Not long ago, I prayed with Carolyn concerning a decision that we needed to make; both of us were bewildered, frustrated, and emotionally spent. I wanted to provide answers, giving Carolyn a sense of security, but all I could do was ask God to shed light on our utter confusion. Confessing my total dependence upon him, we simply told God our needs. Later, when God did send an answer, I knew that my decision to be vulnerable had helped lead us to his will.

Joy

Prayer also erupts from thankful hearts. Dave and Robin say that their times of united prayer are often "fairly spontaneous—when we are rejoicing over something!"

Transformation

God changes us through prayer. As Connor attests: "Praying with Judi has taught me to be humble. As a husband, sometimes I feel like I can't be subordinate or I should always be under control and in charge. When I pray, I realize how much God is in control of everything and that I should only trust him."

The process of prayer is encompassed by paradox: It is hard work, and yet it's indescribable and empowering in its outworking. Two come to pray, and yet the hearts are united as one. The words spoken out loud are concrete, and yet the change—both initial and ongoing—simply cannot be described, categorized, or explained.

. . . .

How would you rate your couple prayer life? Don't base your answer on how often you pray, who leads, or how long your prayer time lasts. For now, forget the time issue. How have you both been changed by prayer—together?

. . . .

Prayer may be the single most empowering gift that God grants us as couples. Yet we confess to feeling guilt in this area also, for we do not utilize this gift as we should. Maybe at this juncture it's important to take in Karl and Sharon's insightful comments: "We've found that the process has been far more important than keeping records of the time span. We're sure that there have been times when the hours spent in prayer were small and others when it was more. But the genuineness is more important than the quantity."

Process versus duration. Being changed within rather than rote action without. Authenticity over quantity. Let's not dismiss the need to pray more, but at the same time, we can focus on a new goal for our prayers: to deepen our relationship with God in a way that changes us to be more like him. That's what God is interested in.

PRAYER AS A PATTERN

As we said earlier, couples have a tendency to model their methods of spiritual growth after what they do as individuals. For generations we've had this unrealistic image that we tried to follow. But not one of the couples we surveyed was happy with trying to adapt their individual devotions to their shared spiritual growth. Maybe you've seen great success in reading and studying the Bible together. If so, you are in a rare minority! But if you are one of those unfulfilled couples, there's a much more effective approach, one that is modeled after the spiritual discipline of prayer.

Let's look once again at some of the interviewees' recurring comments about prayer:

- Prayer brings a certain oneness.
- Prayer allows us to reveal our hearts to the Lord.
- Praying together literally held us together.
- Prayer teaches us lessons about ourselves, our feelings, and our strengths.
- In prayer, we unite our hearts and our minds— which then unites us before him.
- When we pray together we expose everything to God.
- The process of prayer has been far more important than the length of time we spend doing it.

Evidently, the process of prayer just naturally pushes us to do what we as couples need to do: become more intimate with each other and with God. Sharing feelings, revealing and uniting hearts, "exposing" ourselves or becoming vulnerable—all of those components mean that true oneness, unity, and intimacy are taking place. Then—and this is part of the mysterious and miraculous—the couple is united in their focus and worship of God. In this position, we now have the exciting potential to experience growth and change.

This then should be our model, not just in prayer, but in our desire to grow together in every way. Therefore, rather than forcing ourselves to sit down to do a study when our feelings and hearts are not united, doesn't it make more sense to focus on communicating with intent and intensity? We're not talking about shallow discussion; nor are we intimating that mere communication about the facts of the day will cause deep spiritual growth. Instead, we're calling for an intentional and intense process with a specific goal in mind: intimacy with each other that naturally flows toward deep relationship with God. More and more, we're convinced that's a God-designed process.

··

What do you think *intent* and *intensity* mean for your relationship? Describe them in terms of communication. If we define *intent* as a deliberate scheduling of a regular time together and *intensity* as a commitment to deep communication that promotes intimacy, how could you apply those definitions to your communication as a couple? In what ways can you grow in this area?

··

In private prayer there is an unexplainable process that occurs when a child of God comes to him with a repentant, vulnerable, pliable heart, and the Holy Spirit moves to make deep change possible. That pattern is echoed in a couple's shared spiritual growth as two become one in ever-increasing vulnerability and trust. We've known that to happen time and time again, and so have the couples we interviewed.

The fascinating dichotomy that we observed, however, is this: The couples we interviewed rarely made the connection that it was their times of intimacy—sharing hearts and being vulnerable on a walk, through a crisis, or on the way to the grocery store—that were directly connected to their spiritual growth. They segregated what they considered "spiritual" (praying or reading the Bible) from the "secular" (deep communication). Communicating was something they not only desired but also sought intuitively and naturally.

The final irony was that the interviewees felt frustrated in their desire for more time for communication while feeling tremendous guilt for not practicing the expected model of couple devotions. No wonder they felt defeated. It must be like swimming upstream, against the current—when downstream was where you wanted to go after all! As we read story after story, however, we had the incredible perspective of watching the intimate conversations flow right into spiritual growth as a couple.

Rick and Tracy give us an exact illustration of this: "Talking is our main path of growth in our marriage, both spiritually and otherwise. We have always been intrigued by conversation with one another, and we share very often on many levels of intimacy." And how do they follow up that statement—just moments later? "We have only read the Bible together a few times in our marriage. We feel guilty and frustrated that this is true!"

We think it's time to give Rick and Tracy—and perhaps you and your spouse—a break from the guilt. Your instincts and felt needs are neither wrong nor misguided! Instead, you've been heading in the right direction all along—seeking in-depth communication—and we now would like to excuse you from your assumptions about couple devotions. As a matter of fact, we'd like to make this an official edict:

YOU MAY NOW SEEK SPIRITUAL GROWTH AS A COUPLE
WITH INTENT AND INTENSITY THROUGH DEEP COMMUNICATION.

Official enough? Good.

And before you begin thinking this is going to be a piece of cake, you'd best think again. Spiritual growth never comes easy; it's hard work that calls for sacrifice, commitment, and change. Your mom's advice that "anything worthwhile doesn't come easy" was right on target after all. We're not offering an "Easy to Do—Easy to Change!" ten-step plan.

Instead, we're going to begin focusing on those two major qualifying words: *intent* and *intensity.* Ready to really dig in? Better get your work clothes on.

lampposts to our souls

Can Our Emotions Lead Us to God?

eelings and emotions. Are they nemeses or friends…liabilities or strengths…burdens or gifts? In the course of an hour, I (Carolyn) think I've experienced them to be every single one of those! But no matter what we may think or feel, this truth remains: We are created in God's image, Jesus demonstrated that he was a feeling person, and our emotions are given to us as gifts indeed. Somehow we need to come to accept and even be grateful for these "gifts," seeing them as a unique and special part of God's human creation.

I imagine that it didn't take the two of you long (maybe by the second date?) to discover that you are quite different in regard to your emotional makeup. One of you is probably termed "more emotional," although that could very well be either one of you. In our marriage, the creative, artistic, and right-brained side of this partnership is me (Carolyn). Craig and I have learned that I need to talk through and process my deep emotions; if I don't, they'll resurface time and time again—sometimes in the most inopportune and unrelated ways. Craig just loves it when that happens. Needless to say, we've gained a high respect for my emotional needs!

Even though my feelings seem to be deeper, more frequent, and more obvious to others than Craig's, we've learned that his emotions do have equal value and importance—even though they may not be as apparent as mine. We've also recognized that Craig has a tendency to subconsciously delay the expression of his feelings, possibly not even learning of their existence until days after the initial feeling-producing event.

As one who used to focus solely on the rational—and who had little regard for the emotional—Craig has changed dramatically in his appreciation and respect for the emotional part of our relationship. Though we both used to merely tolerate each other's feelings (for greatly differing reasons), we would agree that we now attempt to embrace them.

If you've been one who has a tendency to disregard the value of your own (or others') emotions, then hear this: *Feelings are important.* First of all, they were created by God, and anything molded by his hands has intrinsic worth. As for their substance, they can be nearly indescribable murmurings, overwhelming bursts, or even submerged controllers that direct a person's actions. But no matter how we experience them or to what depth, whether they are denied, ignored, stuffed, or even feared, this fact remains: They are potent forces to be reckoned with, able to intimidate and dominate us. How then do we move from being controlled by our emotions to finding power in and over them?

We believe that feelings are the "lampposts to our souls," and because of that, they are incredible tools—signals—that point us toward where we need to grow in our intimacy with God and each other. But before we can move past the fears and stop being intimidated by these sometimes unmanageable and out-of-control feelings, we have to understand what emotions are—and are not.

EMOTIONS JUST ARE

It's easy to assign value to an emotion, automatically labeling it as good or bad. But feelings just…*are.* A core emotion has no morality in itself.

It's not evil, wrong, or sinful to feel a spark of something, whether it be anger, jealousy, pride—or joy, peace, thankfulness. Every part of humankind has indeed been affected by the Fall; our emotions, intellect, spirit, and soul all died the day that Adam and Eve sinned. In that respect, all emotions are tainted. But so is our intellect! Why are we skeptical only of our emotions when we need to make a decision? Haven't we all at least once reasoned that feelings can be dangerous and therefore should be mistrusted and discounted, and that we need to use our intellect alone to make wise decisions? However, it's a double standard to judge feelings to be sinful while the intellect is regarded as an untainted and reliable guide.

When we experience anything from a near accident, listening to our child recount a painful experience at school, or witnessing an act of injustice, we feel something—instantly. That suddenly ignited spark cannot be stopped or managed in any way. It's a revelation of the core of who and what we are. And doesn't God continually reassure us in his Word that he loves us exactly as we are? Amazingly, we're told that he loved us "while we were yet sinners" (Romans 5:8, NASB).

If an aggressive driver runs me off the road, then I (Carolyn) will certainly feel intensely angry. That's a feeling that "just is." But if I then decide to feed that emotion by focusing on what the driver has done, mulling over the despicable act until I've worked my emotions into a frenzy and possibly even plotting an imaginative revenge, then I've moved into an area of immorality. That is a sin. Needless to say, speaking or acting out my anger in an uncontrolled way would also be wrong. But the initial feeling of anger? That just is. There is a vast difference between that instant feeling and a decision to feed an emotion with sinful thoughts. For far too long Christians have felt guilt over those instant feelings plus many other emotions that we've erroneously labeled as sinful.

Anger simply *is* when it's felt instantly after a cutting remark uttered by a spouse, when we see a small child bullied at the playground, when we hear a prejudiced comment. Can you imagine how potentially freeing this concept can be? Picture how much easier it would be to share with each other intimately—at a time designed just for this purpose—if we're released from the pressure to feel only "good or acceptable emotions."

•••

Do you find it hard to accept that feelings just are? Think of a time when you felt deep guilt about an instant feeling. Now imagine that same feeling as having no moral consequence...and concentrate on letting go of that guilt. Share this incident with your spouse.

•••

Try to grasp being freed from guilt for feelings that are uninvited, uncontrollable, or that come unbidden, sometimes at the most inappropriate times. If we can accept this concept, then we can turn our attention and focus to the next step: what to do when feelings turn into wrong behavior—when we intentionally fuel them, when we allow them to fester into bitterness, when we speak or act in a sinful way.

FEELINGS ARE SIGNALS

When an exuberant puppy first begins to listen and obey, the trainer advances from feeling totally out of control and being at the pup's mercy to thinking, "Finally! Now I'm in charge!" (Well, possibly. Our black lab has always known who's really in charge in our home: She is.) The same is true for our emotions. When we continue to think of them as sinful, something to be feared, or that which makes us feel totally out of control when we admit their existence, then ironically, they do indeed control us. Yet, in actuality, there is tremendous potential here, for God planned for our emotions to be incredible tools because they are signals. Our job is to learn how to listen to their messages.

A "red-light" feeling would include anger, sadness, and fear, while "green-light" feelings include peace, happiness, and security. Each "light" is signaling that something is happening inside us. Whether that surface feeling is pleasing or not, it's still a sign of something occurring deeper within. And this is when the detective work begins. Whenever we note an uncomfortable feeling of any kind—insecurity, rejection, or irritation, for example—then we have the opportunity to look deep inside, to use this signaling emotion and attempt to discover the origin of that feeling.

Not long ago, I (Carolyn) was on my morning walk when I noticed my prayers were constantly being distracted by strong feelings of insecurity. It was as if a blanket of anxiety shadowed me along that pathway, coloring the scenery, my heart, and my outlook on life. I would soon be speaking at a retreat, and I was a bit tense and stressed about that. But the anxiety I was experiencing went beyond normal ranges—even for me! As I searched for the feelings beneath the feeling of insecurity, I encountered pure fear. Fear of embarrassment, humiliation. (I was struggling with some physical problems at that time, which could make those feelings a reality.)

And then suddenly all that was happening underneath became clear. Though I understood that the word *good* in "God causes all things to work together for good" (Romans 8:28, NASB) means "being transformed to his image" (and sometimes that transforming can indeed be painful), I was not transferring that same understanding to my prayers about trusting God.

On the contrary, when I looked ahead to the retreat and my trusting God for that, I wanted the same type of selfish "good" that too many of us erroneously claim—that it would be good (not embarrassing or humiliating, but productive) for me. With tears of shame, I asked for forgiveness and the willingness to trust him for the better good: that I might be transformed to his image, no matter what that might mean in relation to possible embarrassment. And then I placed myself in the hands of a loving God. I can't say that the fear completely disappeared, but at the same time I was flooded with feelings of peace. Amazingly, those feelings seemed to overwhelm the insecurities because I'd been so vividly reminded that I could trust my God.

....

Can you recall a recent strong feeling that signaled an even deeper feeling? Review your strongest feelings for the week; then practice utilizing those surface feelings to reveal what's buried underneath. How can you use this process to help each other draw nearer to God?

....

In this illustration, we see how emotions can be lampposts to our relationship with God. If I had disregarded the feelings, felt shame for them, and then pushed them into hiding or even merely concentrated on the emotions alone—fueling them with no constructive plan to view them as signals for something amiss happening within—then I would have missed the opportunity to grow in my understanding of who God is and how intimately he loves me. When emotions are viewed in this light, they do have incredible power *for* us rather than *over* us!

FEELINGS AND SPIRITUAL GROWTH AS A COUPLE

Understanding our feelings as lampposts can offer opportunities for tremendous individual growth. But it can also make a difference in how we share during our times of intentional communication.

No Emotion Is Off-Limits

When we think of feelings as lampposts, we have the freedom to share anything and everything that we're feeling because those feelings "just are." We do not judge each other—no matter how awful something might appear.

Years ago, I (Carolyn) covered up some feelings that I considered to be wrong. I didn't tell Craig about the jealousy I felt toward a relative when she had a baby girl. Frankly, I was ashamed to admit that to him. Eventually, I did find the courage and after quickly sharing how miserable I felt, his only response was, "Boy, that's not healthy. You'd better work on that." Needless to say, his remarks seemed judgmental and instructive, which didn't help me process the feelings at all; instead, it only added more guilt to my already overloaded conscience.

Today I still feel embarrassed when I need to share uncomfortable feelings, but I know I can expect an accepting and loving response from Craig. Rather than responding judgmentally, I know he will allow me to express whatever I need to and then help me discover the pain that's hidden beneath. What a difference! Now things that are difficult to share are actually potential chances for greater intimacy rather than a concern of "Will he still love me if I admit this?"

Were I to experience that same jealousy today, I know that Craig's response would be one of concern. I can hear him asking, "Sweetheart, where do you think those feelings are coming from? How can I help you uncover the hidden hurt that you evidently are feeling underneath that feeling of jealousy?" Rather than a guilt-producing exchange between us, I'm confident that now Craig would help me to know myself—and God—better.

••

Can you think of a feeling—maybe experienced this week—that you're embarrassed to share with your spouse? Can you "mine" that feeling and determine what it reveals about your concept of God? Share your insights with your mate.

••

Many of the couples we interviewed talked about this same type of experience, even though they may not have recognized exactly what that experience was about. Laura and John shared that the deaths of both of their fathers over the last few years had been times of crisis. "When John was dealing with his dad's illness," Laura said, "some of his own [John's] fears of death and the unfairness of it all [surfaced]. We were able to talk through the spiritual issues in a way that was helpful to both of us." Note the invaluable connection of honesty, vulnerability, sharing of those deep feelings (which may have been hard to do, considering some might judge them as being "unspiritual"), and the way in which Laura and John ultimately grew spiritually as a couple.

Other couples shared this same desire for intimacy and acceptance when they admitted, "Genuine openness and vulnerability have helped us to grow spiritually," and "Self-disclosure has provided some of our most meaningful times together." It's a process that works—tough as it may be to do, and risky as it may feel.

Emotions Point to Spiritual Issues

Next we help each other discover what's happening underneath...and what we need to learn about our great God. I (Carolyn) determined that my jealousy over the baby girl's birth stemmed from an incorrect understanding of God: I thought he denied my desires for a girl out of a "you'll learn from this if I make you" type of sovereignty. I saw him as a detached and withdrawn God, one who merely watched as an uncaring bystander when I hurt. Those were subconscious and incorrect concepts of God that I carried for years, and all because I was afraid to truly look beneath the feelings that signaled their presence.

Feelings Aren't Weapons

We also don't use our feelings as clubs to beat up each other. When we need to confront a spouse, spitting out "You made me feel hurt!" is not an acceptable approach. Ultimately, I am responsible for my feelings, and I have no right to blame anyone else. "Feelings just are" doesn't give either of us the excuse to fling them at each other like weapons.

I (Craig) can remember very well when I would emphatically say to Carolyn, "I feel that you need to…" and proceed to browbeat her with whatever was bothering me and whatever I was sure she needed to change. Worse yet, I pronounced it as though it were a justifiable and God-given right for me to do that under my understanding of my position in the home! In reality, I was not at all sharing a feeling with her. In prefacing my comments with "I feel that," I was really expressing a judgment, and the word *feel* was an inappropriate word choice.

Too often we confuse the use of the words *judge* and *feel*. "I feel" should always be followed by an emotion like tired, happy, frustrated, or bored. Using "I feel that" is incorrect; instead, the true nature of what we're attempting to express is a viewpoint or conclusion—sometimes accurate, sometimes not. Most important, the difference between merely sharing an emotion—as opposed to judging another (under the false guise of "I feel"), putting your spouse on the defensive—can make a dramatic difference in the effectiveness of your communication. And, guys, if you find yourself using that phrase, you'd best at least change your word choice to "I judge that…" After reading this section, I doubt that you'll get away with misusing the word *feel* in that way again!

•••

Can you grasp the significant difference between saying "I judge that you need to…" and "I feel that you need to…"? Practice using each one in a sentence—correctly.

•••

Respond to Feelings with Love

Sharing a deep feeling can be incredibly hard…and how Carolyn receives it will then determine whether I share more—or less. Attempts to handle each other's feelings with tenderness and love are therefore incredibly important to deeper communication.

Sometimes when Carolyn has confronted me, I have felt instantly defensive. I've then attempted to parry the criticism by deflecting it back onto her. When she points out that I've been unresponsive to her needs or neglected to compliment her, thus making her feel less than cherished, I have quipped back, "Yeah, well, I'm just the worst husband ever!" This is nothing more than an unfair attempt on my part to make her feel bad for sharing her feelings on the issue. I know very well, though, that my response—whether defensive or openly accepting— will determine the depth of her sharing and where that discussion will then take us.

· ·

Discuss with each other whether you have the courage to share a red-light feeling such as anger, fear, or insecurity. Why or why not? If this is still too difficult, what is holding you back?

· ·

After many years of successful parrying (she used to fall for my clever tactic and then attempt to justify her complaint!), I've found that now I can only use it in jest. Carolyn will simply respond, "Good effort. Today maybe you *are* the worst husband in the world. Now can we discuss my feelings on this?"

VULNERABILITY, TRUST, AND BEING REAL

A symbolic picture of submission to authority might be to envision yourself kneeling, head bowed, arms and hands out with the palms open and up. Place your entire self-esteem in those open palms, and you have a picture of complete vulnerability. That's what it's like to lovingly present a tough feeling to a spouse—one you're embarrassed to admit exists, one that only compounds an already brewing feeling of insecurity. But when that feeling is then lovingly accepted and embraced by a spouse, the foundation of trust between the two of you is reinforced in indelible ways. For it's built on unconditional love, and that is the bedrock of deeper intimacy.

This type of experience—the courage to share my feelings by being vulnerable, and to trust that my spouse will handle my feelings with love—is one that is...

- planted with the correct presuppositions, such as the complete freedom to share any feeling, as discussed in the section above.
- cultivated with gentle reminders when necessary.
- nurtured regularly over weeks, months, years.
- encouraged to grow by sharing deeper and tougher feelings with each other as the years go by.

We've found that the continual nurturing of this area of our relationship—deep-level trust—then provides a foundation that supports us when we enter tumultuous times. It's almost as though we've written our own living history book on trust, and we can take that out and "read" it whenever we need to.

Real trust takes time. We entered our marriage with a naive trust. That simplistic level was based merely on our dating and engagement period and all of our spoken promises, which had yet to withstand the tests that life would bring. But as the years went by, as we weathered the tests of integrity and honesty, as we felt the very real pressures to be what we said we were as we lived our lives before our sons, trust was built, layer upon layer, experience upon experience, failure and hurt upon confession and healing.

I (Craig) remember all too well the time when I was released from a job due to financial exigency at the organization where I worked. I'm a conscientious person, one who absolutely desires to do a job well for my family and myself, for the organization I'm employed by, and mostly, for God. I want to provide for Carolyn and my family—not just adequately, but well. So when I began to feel inadequate, powerless, and insecure, I was afraid to face those emotions myself—let alone before Carolyn.

All these feelings were in direct juxtaposition to the self-assured image I usually present to others. Likewise, my true inner self is normally secure and confident. *Would admitting my feelings of inadequacy make Carolyn feel even more insecure herself?* I wondered. *Would Carolyn see me as less of a man? Would she still trust in me as a provider?*

We'd been sharing on Saturday mornings for nearly ten years when this life-changing experience occurred. Tough emotions had been put into the "sapling" of our deep-level trust for enough years to grow it to the strength of a more mature tree; the responses throughout had been wrapped in unconditional acceptance.

This time was no exception. The trust was there, and because of that I had the courage to be honest with Carolyn. Her response? Tenderness and great love. Somehow, though I expected that my revelation would make her feel less secure, she admitted freely that she felt even *more* secure. By inviting Carolyn into my innermost world, we could now face this challenging and frightening experience as a true team. By trusting her, she returned intimate trust to me.

We also want to emphasize the absolute need for both spouses to attempt to be completely real before each other. Obviously, this requires honesty and transparency before God and yourself before you can then be real to your spouse. But if you're ever going to learn how to be vulnerable and intimate, if you're going to build deep trust, if you're going to grow as individuals and as a couple in your relationship with God, then you must begin to see yourselves as you truly are. And that, as we all know, takes trust in a God who accepts and loves us just as we are.

Allen and Eileen exhibit an incredible depth of realness and vulnerability—individually before God, to each other, and to us: "We talk about when we feel close and distant to God and why. When we feel like failures and when we feel 'successful.' When we feel we 'get it' and when we don't know what the Lord is trying to teach us." That's intimacy in process.

I (Carolyn) recall the time an acquaintance told me about intentionally not inviting another friend of hers to a party. She was reveling in the fact that all the others who had been invited had expressed that they didn't want that particular person attending. With great indignity and judgment—oh yes, I even openly admitted my lofty attitude to Craig!— I recounted the entire story to him, explaining the details, imagining the hurt that the excluded woman must be feeling. "Wasn't it awful that while supposedly encouraging the friendships with the other women, she was actually blatantly proving her inability to love unconditionally? In an ironic and backward way, she was alienating those 'friends' just as much as the one she rejected," I mused. "Oh, how awful!"

••

Be painfully honest: Do you have the courage to look at yourself as you really are? Does your spouse agree with your view of yourself? What does that reveal about how you accept God's unconditional love for you?

••

That was our discussion on one Saturday, but by the next weekend, my attitude was just a tinge different. For during prayer that week, I discovered that through an entirely separate incident, I also clearly displayed the same lack of love when I inwardly rejoiced over the criticism of another—and praise of me. In a warped way, I also was signaling not the unconditional love that I desire to give others but conditional love, based on performance. With great humility, I then told Craig what this experience and week of reflection had taught me about my weaknesses, my needs, and God's forgiveness.

Being real—seeking to see myself as I truly am—and then admitting that to God and to my spouse is never going to be easy. We would be defrauding you to say otherwise. Analogies in the Bible speak of Christ as "the Light of the world" and trials being like "fires." Both reveal truth (and he is the Truth) and a need for cleansing, neither being a pleasant process. But each also brings about spiritual growth, maturing, edification. Is not the pain worth the end result?

We're convinced that is so, and therefore our constant goal is to find reality—and to share that with each other constantly and consistently. Drew and Kathy have sought and known this joy too, as Drew shares: "We talk about trust issues and faith issues—about doubt, mission, jealousy, hurt, depression, and dreams. I guess what I have with Kathy is someone to be totally free with. I can be heretical, despondent, inspired, or just pensive, and she understands it. We prize honesty and tend to use that metric for analyzing our spiritual progress."

When deep and honest communication—even painful revelations—are nestled in the atmosphere of unconditional love and trust, the vulnerability is absolutely worth the outcome: greater intimacy.

guidelines, ground rules, and great expectations

How Do We Strengthen Our Communication?

nce I (Carolyn) manage to pry open my eyes on a dreary, rainy morning, I usually focus on one major goal: coffee. Groping my way through the morning routines and then shuffling down the stairs, I head to the kitchen, all the while pretty much operating on autopilot. Even in that near-comatose state, however, there are certain presuppositions that I bring to the process. For example, as groggy as I am, I still know that coffee essentially consists of (1) coffee and (2) water, each plopped into easily marked areas of the coffeepot in varying proportions. I and most other early-morning, caffeine-addicted adults can stumble through that operation even when we're still 99 percent asleep.

But now, *good* coffee...ahhh. That's another matter entirely as Craig the Coffee Connoisseur would say. (He gently shoves me aside at this point to make The Coffee. First thing in the morning, coffee's top priority means it should be in capital letters.) Truly good coffee begins with fresh, newly ground beans and cold water, all put into a good quality coffeepot in just the right proportions. By Craig. I must grudgingly admit that's the start of a very good Saturday morning in the Williford household.

In the same way, we realize that over the years we've developed quite a list of guidelines that give our times together a certain shape and form. Some of these developed out of the people we are and the needs that we bring to this relationship. Other rules, like a strong commitment to this scheduled time together, came about through trial and error, and sometimes, missteps and hurt feelings.

From all our mistakes and rebounds, our lessons learned and classes taught, these are the presuppositions, rules, and expectations that we bring to our Saturday morning time together. We've found each one to be absolutely vital to its success.

A Commitment to Weekly Time Together

Have you noticed that life is crammed full of too many good things? For instance, does anyone care to venture a guess as to how many men's meetings are scheduled for Saturday mornings? Well, that's easy. All of them are! And at every church we've attended, I (Craig) have been encouraged to come to not merely one but generally several of these worthwhile gatherings. I'd just get past the phone calls ("Why can't you come? You do *what* on Saturday mornings?") and subtle pressure ("But surely you can do that another day; this is important!") when yet another men's group would start up.

I quickly set about redirecting the questions in fairly creative ways. I suppose my personal favorite was my response to the "But you need to set an example!" line. I'd simply grin and say, "I *am* setting an example; I'm showing everyone how much I love my wife!" Now I want to go on record as noting that these meetings were indeed worthwhile, but sometimes as Christians we're faced with choosing between *two good things*. Because of my commitment to *us*, I determined to choose that good over the other.

I (Carolyn) have also had the dilemma of choosing between two "goods." We'd been at this for many years when I had an exciting opportunity to sing in a musical at church. There was only one major drawback: The rehearsals would be held on Saturday mornings, for months. Now throughout the years, there were countless times when we had to shift our Saturday morning time together to another day. We will freely admit that it must've sounded rather strange to overhear us say something like, "Well, then, let's have Saturday morning on Friday this week, okay? Good." However, when the opportunity to sing in the musical came along, we were in a particularly busy period. Our morning simply could not be changed, since we were already struggling with finding time because of our sons' various activities on the weekends. Admittedly being rather righteous and just a tinge put-out, I turned down the musical. (First million-dollar question: Can you detect just a slight attitude developing?)

Soon after that an opportunity came along for me to participate in another production; that one-time rehearsal was also on a Saturday morning, and I eagerly and immediately committed to it—without discussing this decision with Craig. I mean, hadn't I already made the ultimate sacrifice by turning down the big musical? So what was the big deal about our missing just one Saturday? Well, who would've guessed Craig would get so bent out of shape over one little misstep! (Second million-dollar question: Can you guess what confrontational issue we discussed that next Saturday morning?)

Now that we look back, it's amazing how many things—good things—competed for our Saturday mornings. All types of activities our sons were in—every sport imaginable, church and school activities, and the seemingly endless practices for each of those—all demanded time, as you who are parents know too well. And all too often they were scheduled for, of course, Saturday morning.

I remember apprehensively watching when one of the guys would come home from school on a Friday, dump his backpack on the table, reach into its fathomless depths, and pull out a crumpled sheet with *Important: Schedule* written across the top. I just knew the word *Saturday* was going to be on there somewhere.

BEING FLEXIBLE AND CREATIVE

The only way we managed to salvage our Saturdays during those years was by being flexible and adaptable. We'd take a long evening walk together around the neighborhood, find another morning to squeeze in our special time, go out to eat one night that week—just the two of us—or even shoo our guys out of the family room on Saturday afternoon so we had a few hours to ourselves.

Still, we missed many Saturdays over the years. Sometimes two in a row. But believe me, we felt it when we did; there was definitely a deficit in our communication, compassion, understanding, and ability to just plain get along. As a matter of fact, were we to chart our major arguments, there's no doubt that the majority of them occurred when we'd not had our regular Saturday morning time together for two or more consecutive weeks. Needless to say, we honestly have not missed two weeks in a row that often over these last twenty-plus years. Not only do we desperately desire that time together…but we've learned how desperately we need it.

MOVING FROM DESIRE TO NEED

And that leads us to state this without reservation: What started as a "we should do this" quickly became a deep desire. That desire then developed into a need. It is much easier to commit to those things in our lives that we see as absolute needs. I (Craig) have no problem viewing eating as a need; no one—and especially not my sons when it comes to the subject of our family's traditional lasagna on Christmas Day—would say *that* commitment is lacking in my life! But the serious point is this: We don't lose time or energy debating about the need to eat. We don't generally forget or allow other activities to crowd out mealtimes. We simply *do it* because it's necessary and good!

Therefore, when our time to talk grew into that kind of felt need, we developed an attitude of fierce protectiveness toward it. We both had a deep desire for connecting in that deeper way. Youth basketball games on Saturday mornings? We'll do that if we must, but we'll find another time for us every week until that season is over. A church meeting scheduled for Saturday morning? If at all possible—and generally this was more easily done than one might imagine—I (Craig) rescheduled it to another day or a later time on Saturday. As a matter of fact, it was amazing what could be shifted *with enough determination on our part.* It just took the effort, backed by the desire to have a felt need fulfilled.

We added one more motivation to our desire for deep and honest communication that also led to the recognition of an intense need for uninterrupted Saturday mornings. Just out of college and ever so green, we headed off to our first full-time pastorate. We'd only been there about a year when we learned that one of the pastors in our association was having an affair with a counselee.

I (Carolyn) remember feeling deeply saddened by this, but even more, I recall the nearly quaking fear of insecurity that the news seemed to throw over my spirit. I can clearly picture where we were and the exact conversation that ensued when Craig and I discussed the devastation of this incident.

"I can't believe he would do that," I said.

"Sweetheart, it could happen to anyone."

"Don't say that! Saying *anyone* means it could happen to us!"

"Yes, it *could* happen to us. And that's exactly why we must always be proactive in our relationship, guarding against that very thing in our marriage."

We tell couples in premarital counseling that we operate by a paradox: Losing our relationship is not an option for us. When we married, we agreed to never use the word *divorce* in jest nor throw it at each other as a threat when angry. But at the same time we believe we *could* lose each other, so we do everything in our power to keep that from happening. It's unthinkable and, in our marriage, unspeakable. But we both still recognize that it could happen.

. . . .

Do you both agree that divorce could happen to you? If so, then does that give you a sense of urgency to proactively work on your marriage? Why or why not?

. . . .

Maybe it's not hard to understand then why we've clung to our Saturday mornings as though they were a lifeline. In a real sense, they comprise the thread woven throughout our years together, taking us through transitions, conflict, stress, confusion, pain, and ultimately—incredible spiritual growth as a couple. All the commitment and flexibility would pay off in a relationship that moved us not only closer to each other but also to God. We can't imagine what our lives would have been like without devoting ourselves to each other on Saturdays.

Drew and Kathy express this same kind of deep desire for communication in their marriage: "Our best times of growth and encouragement come through the everyday issues of life. We talk constantly—almost every day, sometimes for hours—about what God is doing in our lives and with us." *Talking constantly.* Who would have thought conversation would be such a driving force for spiritual growth?

When an activity becomes that much of a need…when the evidences of benefit are that apparent…when intimacy happens month after month…then you *make* it happen.

Listening Is Active

When we picture someone talking, we obviously visualize action: The mouth is moving, and if the person is animated, hands and arms are most likely busy too! But when we imagine someone listening, we probably envision no movement at all. Very likely we'd picture the person holding absolutely still; that would indicate that he or she is really concentrating. Therefore, we'd probably conclude that speaking is active while listening is passive, but nothing could be further from the truth.

In reality, too often we are not listening to the other person, even when we're quiet and maintaining eye contact. Instead, we may be mentally preparing our response or in the case of conflict, structuring our defense. For example, have you ever noticed a tendency to completely miss a person's name during an introduction? That's because you were not actively listening; instead, you were concentrating on the impression you were making at that moment.

We could also easily be preoccupied with other events in our lives, our minds tracking to another issue we're concerned about. Or even something as simple as movement just outside a window. The problem is, we generally are *not* good listeners; we mistakenly think it is relatively easy to do, doesn't take effort on our parts, and mostly, we're lackadaisical about the process because we consider listening passive.

Listening is actually a hidden or subconscious activity. Some of the elements that make one a good listener are not readily apparent, while others are more obvious. First, the listener is proactively determined to focus on what the other person is saying rather than on her own response. Her energy is directed toward the speaker's heart, revealed through the spoken words. Second, an active listener is aware of several forms of nonverbal communication. Giving direct eye contact and positive body posture, she conveys her involvement in the conversation (no crossed arms to block intimacy, and her body is faced toward the one sharing in an open and encouraging stance). Third, the listener often restates what she's taking in to assure her spouse that she's hearing the message accurately—or maybe allowing her to realize that no, she has not. (In which case, the message needs to be repeated until the listener can restate it—correctly.) And finally, an active listener is intent on making the other person feel valued, respected, and worthy of being heard.

••

We also need to actively listen to God. Do you regularly determine to quiet your mind, stop the rushed pace of life for a while, and attempt to discern God's leading? Would a day of fasting help you to achieve this goal? With your spouse, discuss other creative ways you can listen to God's prompting—as individuals and as a couple.

••

Do these seem overstated? We have to be honest and admit that we thought so when we first heard these suggestions. But our worst offenses were in the areas of preparing a response or defense. When we both finally began to concentrate on proactively listening to what the other was saying, it made an incredible difference not only in our listening skills with each other but also with everyone in our circle of influence.

Other couples note the importance of listening skills too, as evidenced by this comment from Stan and Jean: "We've both learned to understand God in a deeper way through unconditional love, accepting each other no matter what, and listening." That tie of "unconditional love and acceptance" and "listening" is not accidental; the two are inherently joined.

In relation to nonverbal signals, I (Craig) had to admit that arms crossed over my chest was often an "I'm feeling defensive" position that would push Carolyn away rather than invite her in. And if I'm distracted by an animal in the pine meadow behind our home, Carolyn is quick to ask (with a teasing smile, I should add), "*Hello?* Are you with me?"

....

What are some of the ways you have been a passive listener in the past? How have you discouraged your spouse from sharing more? How can you both improve in this area and thereby strengthen your communication?

....

Active listening is not an oxymoron, and in actuality, these rules for listening call for practice, consistency, and an attitude that clings to their importance and viability. Do we sometimes mess up? Oh, absolutely. But in my defense, when I'm distracted and catch a glimpse of rusty red fur dashing through the meadow outside, we both agree to a short time-out. Even during a heated discussion, Carolyn will readily take a break to watch a red fox. Every once in a while, rules are meant to be broken!

THE PLANETS WE COME FROM

Several years ago, books about how men and women relate became instantly popular as they "proved" that the sexes could never really understand each other because they're so vastly different. Others picked up on that theme and enhanced it even more, but the concept was nothing new, and we guys knew that. For the theory that men and women—and even husbands and wives—can never relate in a deep way because of inherent differences has been around forever. If you don't believe me, then just ask the oldest man you know this question: "So, do *you* understand women?"

Admittedly, I used to completely buy that idea. And that age-old assumption was the driving force behind my excuses to never...

- wade into the uncomfortable and unfathomable arena of Carolyn's feelings.
- grant that her "female intuition" might have something to it after all.
- admit to my having feelings; that was her thing and we couldn't be anything alike.
- really be vulnerable and, therefore, intimate.

The women versus men scenario lent itself to all kinds of handy excuses on my part. *After all,* I'd reason, *why even attempt to understand my wife if that's an impossible task anyway?*

But eventually I realized that I was merely using that tired line as an easy out; it was a way to shirk my responsibility to know Carolyn intimately—her heart, her thoughts, her feelings. Sure, we are different in so many ways. But that does nothing to negate how we are alike: We both feel emotions, and the feeling of rejection is rejection, whether felt by a male or female. We both need intimacy, and that can only be achieved by being vulnerable enough to share deeply. And we both were created as spiritual beings in need of God and his grace. Certainly, there are countless other ways that we *are* alike; therefore, to concentrate on the differences is counterproductive. Isn't it time we stopped using that excuse—which is really no more than a cover for our laziness and cowardice—and instead seek in-depth communication and understanding of our spouses?

Daryl proudly states—as he indeed should—that he and Kim talk about "even the things some of the scholars and professionals say that men shouldn't discuss with their wives. We also talk about the things that men want to discuss—but wives supposedly can't understand or take the wrong way. I would say this is one of the strongest points of our relationship. I just can't keep my mouth shut concerning my thoughts!"

Good for Daryl. He has discovered what no one besides our great God could even begin to imagine, let alone design: "God created man in his own image, in the image of God he created him; male *and* female he created them" (Genesis 1:27, emphasis added). Man...woman. Likeness...difference. Analogous...unique. It's all God's plan for intimacy.

BEWARE OF PRESUPPOSITIONS

Presuppositions can be tricky to get your hands around. Remember that they're hidden motivators. They guide and control us in both a positive and a negative sense. Craig and I have operated by the guidelines described above for so many years that they've become second nature. But we also realize that new presuppositions can sneak into the subconscious and become a part of our communication "rules" through media, church, and the influence of family, friends, and others whose opinions we value—and maybe those we don't.

The slippery part of presuppositions, however, is this: Exposing them in your marriage is the only way to understand what is actually driving your communication patterns. Seeing them clearly, judging them for what they are, and discussing their value gives you a choice in what will—and will not—motivate and direct your sharing, growth, and intimacy as a couple. Only when the presuppositions are out in the open can you then intentionally decide, *Do we want this to control us? Is this a pattern we like? What do we want to discard? What do we want to keep?*

In the first years of our marriage, I (Carolyn) used the communication tool of *hinting*, a pattern that I learned in my family of origin. I found it to be quite successful within my family, since we all spoke the same "language." But after Craig and I had been married awhile, it appeared to me that Craig was rather slow. At least, it seemed that way, since he sure didn't catch my hints. Or better put: He didn't act on them.

For example, after dinner I might've said something like, "Boy, I sure am tired. I wish I could just lie down and rest awhile." Now, I would've thought I'd hinted pretty clearly that I wanted *him*—and him alone—to do the dishes. But Craig might have responded by saying, "Well, we'd better get these dishes done. We've both had a long day." See what I mean about slow?

But after a few years went by and we got better at communicating, we talked about my hinting as opposed to having the courage to simply express my need. Craig pointed out that he'd always caught my hints through the years; he just wasn't about to respond to them! The presupposition that hinting was an acceptable communication pattern was not one that he wanted us to continue to hold. After understanding the dynamics of hinting as opposed to honesty and directness, I agreed wholeheartedly. But it wasn't until we broke out of that pattern that we were really able to have a choice in what we would continue to use and what we wanted to discard.

Every once in a while, I still slip up. I might hint to Craig something to the effect of "I sure wish this floor were swept." And Craig—ever the direct one—will ask, "Do you want me to sweep the floor?"

I've learned enough by now to respond, "Yes!"

This is an important area to cover in your couple time. But since so many presuppositions are unconscious, here are a few ideas for bringing them to the surface:

- Talk about your families of origin. What communication paterns do you see evidenced there—positive and negative?
- What patterns have you adopted into your new home, maybe merely by habit?
- Consider these possible models and decide if they are ones you are currently using and if you want to continue using them:

pouting, manipulation, the "silent treatment," hinting, domination, coercion, withholding affection, persuasion.

- How will you agree to go about changing, if you both decide that must happen? What steps will you take to make sure you have a decisive plan for progress?

By itself, just one of the "rules" in this chapter may seem insignificant to your time to grow spiritually together. But when you begin practicing all of them with consistency, we think you'll be amazed at how they provide the atmosphere needed to move toward intimacy with each other—and with God.

We've set the stage for your couple time. Your props are all in place. Now it's time for the script.

life's journey provides the script

What Do We Talk About?

henever we talk to other couples about devoting intentional time to each other every week, invariably we are asked: "What on earth do you talk about?" Our pat answer is to jokingly reply that life seems to always provide us with *something* to discuss, but in truth, that is actually the case! It is in the daily-ness of life—its transitions, challenges, and interruptions to normalcy (whatever that is)—that we find much to dissect and debate. And that's how we discover just what God is about in our lives.

Staying in tune with each other in our overscheduled lives can be a challenge. The couples we interviewed repeatedly shared how they creatively utilize times to catch up whenever they can. Don and Rebecca enjoy "going out for coffee—usually when the kids spend the night at Grandma's—and discussing what's happening in our lives." Dave and Robin agree that they talk "whenever we can grab a minute!" So if couples commonly desire more time to talk, and an intentional, planned time would provide that, why is it that we sometimes look at each other and freeze in silence?

One problem is the word *intent*. Too many times we've heard couples complain that "Planned times just don't work for us." Know what? We're not buying that—at least, not the planned time that we're experiencing. Somehow scheduled conversation got a bum rap. It was brought to trial and convicted of being *canned,* and heaven forbid that should be the case. But who says that intentional and planned equal boring? Where did we get the idea that just because our time together is scheduled that it can't lead to in-depth communication and deep intimacy? During our dating years, didn't we "schedule" time just to get to know each other? Back then we called it a date, and we certainly thought that was a great idea!

As of this moment, let's drop the negative connotations that equate *planned* with *canned.* Anyone who's been on a well-organized, researched, and mapped-out vacation knows advance planning can mean the difference between an exciting, fun, and relaxing time and a disorganized mess of dashed expectations. We're firmly convinced that it's what you bring to the time that makes or breaks it: your positive expectations, energy and input, the desire to grow as a couple. As Craig likes to say, "I don't believe God has ever been intimidated by our advance preparations!"

Another benefit to a positive attitude is that couples can approach tough times that way: by seeing the potential to grow closer. Tragedies, transitions, and stresses upon our marriages will always happen. If you're not in one of those right now, just wait a bit! But how we respond to those—whether we'll approach them with an attitude of "How can we grow through this with God's help?" as opposed to "Our marriage can't handle this!" might make all the difference in whether we strengthen our relationship or allow the incident to push us apart. What will your attitude be when the challenges come? Will you take control of the situation, or will you allow the event to control you?

As we've said, the ordinary events and challenges of life tend to supply all the raw material we need for intentional communication and intimacy. The transitions of life are a major part of this. Quite honestly,

I (Carolyn) don't handle transitions well. And as I'm writing this, I can hear Craig thinking, "*That's* certainly the understatement of the year!" At the same time, Kamikaze Change Craig seems to thrive on it. Our reactions to life's transitions are as different as we are.

Job Change?

Craig: Great—a new challenge!

Me: I can't even find your *current* office, for crying out loud.

Moving Across the Country?

Craig: I can't wait! There's so much of this country we haven't seen yet!

Me: If I have to look at *one more box...*

Empty Nest?

Craig: So...where were we anyway?!

Me: Who am I? My babies are gone; am I still a mom?

The Blender Dies?

Craig: Where can we find the cheapest replacement?

Me: But that was the *only* appliance left from our original wedding gifts! Think how old it is—how sentimental! We made milkshakes in it for family nights, remember? We'd toss in *gobs* of chocolate, and the guys were just ecstatic! And then there was the time...

Okay, that's a bit of a stretch, but the point is this: Life is full of change and challenge. Transitions come in one tremendous blow—like a career switch or the birth of a baby—or they may arrive in small snatches that catch you unawares. All that *stuff* provides the beginnings of a great conversation.

Let's work through some of those opportunities, and then we'll give specific examples of questions to spark discussion, should you find yourself in that stage of life.

QUESTIONS FOR WHEREVER YOU ARE RIGHT NOW

You may be going through a period of calm with no significant change; if that's the case, enjoy it while it lasts! Whatever stage of life you're currently facing, there are some topics that float to any situation.

Your Strongest Feeling of the Week
Share the experience, and don't forget to dig beneath the surface feelings to find what's buried within. What might those feelings reveal about your conceptions of God? How can you get inside each other's heart as you share your strongest feelings?

Your Relationship with God
What did you learn in your prayer, study, or journaling this week? What does God seem to be teaching you? Of course these topics hinge on the assumption that you both have an individual time with God on a regular basis. We'll discuss the absolute importance of this in more depth in the next chapter.

Your Favorite Thing Versus the Worst Thing
What was it about the past week that you'd love to erase and do again? What event would you like to savor? How did both of those make you feel—and especially in relation to facing the week ahead?

Where Do You Think You Are As a Couple?
How would you rate your relationship right now: intimately close, doing fairly well, average, plugging along, barely surviving, or not on

the same page? What's contributing to that? What can you do to grow closer right now?

Traditions for Birthdays and Anniversaries
Make the most of these times with a commitment to serious communication. Jim and Renee share that they have several questions they work through on every anniversary:

- What was the most enjoyable event this year?
- What was the hardest thing that happened? How could we have dealt with that better, and what can we learn from that?
- What are the strengths and weaknesses in our marriage?
- What was the funniest thing that happened?
- What goals do we want to set for the upcoming year?

QUESTIONS FOR TIMES OF TRANSITION

There are numerous transitions in our lives—the death of a family member or friend, aging parents, empty nest, retirement, or the transition from preschool kids to the elementary years. The following questions are especially suited for life's transitional periods. These questions will help you work through those times.

Career Changes and Challenges
It could be that you've made a major change in this area, or maybe you've remained in the same job while the workplace has managed to change *around* you. Whatever the case, our careers present significant challenges, problems, and opportunities—and therefore, plenty of subject matter for deep and meaningful communication.

Here are some questions to get you started:

- What are you learning about yourself in your job right now?
- What are your future goals in regard to your career? Dream as big as you want to—and then continue to dream together!

- What event of the week was the most significant to you?
- What did you learn from that—or any other happening from this week?
- What specifically is causing you to stretch and grow the most?
- What's making you feel uncomfortable and why?
- What happened this week that you feel good about?
- What were your successes this week? Your failures? How do each of you feel about those?
- How are you getting along with your immediate supervisors? Your staff?
- How are you feeling overall? Frustrated? Fulfilled? Content? Stressed?

Rick and Tracy "share what we call a 'High-Low.' We tell what our high was that day, and also the low." That could easily be adapted to talking about work situations (or any experience from the week), providing a nugget to send you on a tangent in any direction of discussion! Another couple, Dwayne and Pam, use their respective jobs as catalysts to "talk about the struggles we experience there that may call for us to respond with pretty selfish and sinful reactions; we tend to try to bring each other back to center at such times by gently encouraging the other toward a godly response."

Sometimes work, career, or business triggers a true crisis, and couples told us those intense times pushed them to greater closeness with God and with each other. Serena says that she and Randy "grew together through a family crisis in business; we only had each other and the Lord, so we *had* to leave what we couldn't possibly handle to Him." Dave and Robin have known the pain of career tragedy too: "When we've gone through very difficult times, we've prayed more and really supported each other. Feeling the support and presence of each other carries you through those dark valleys."

One of our most moving and therefore intimate conversations

came as the result of our intense discussions concerning Craig's job. He was going through a particularly stressful time, a period when his integrity was constantly being put to the test—at great personal cost. As he made difficult decisions concerning issues among his staff, many times he had to silently take the blame to protect others. This had been going on for months, and so a frequent topic on our mornings together was Craig's emotions about all of this: his feelings of hurt, frustration, and loneliness. I *thought* I understood—until a situation arose in my life.

My friend Sherry had been deeply wounded due to her husband's sudden loss of a job. Around the same time, other members of our women's group were about to make decisions that would inadvertently profoundly hurt her yet again. They knew of Sherry's plight but did not know the circumstances nor how deep her pain was. I knew I had to protect my friend and decided to go to bat—discovering quickly that my pleas were falling on deaf ears. Eventually, I was forced to battle hard on her behalf, risking my relationship with those women in the process. At the same time, I knew quite well that Sherry would never know about these intense, behind-the-scenes confrontations.

Craig and I came to our next Saturday morning with heavy hearts and the weight of a nightmarish week. As we shared with each other, the house seemed otherwise eerily empty and quiet. Except for my plaintive cry.

"I had to really argue on Sherry's behalf," I complained to Craig, "and I'm just exhausted from the emotional intensity of that. But if they'd carried out those original plans, I just know Sherry would've been deeply hurt. And I couldn't stand by and watch that happen!"

"Then you did the right thing," Craig affirmed.

"But I had to fight so hard for this, and no one involved in that situation will ever know the cost I paid, including Sherry! I'm feeling angry and spent and deeply hurt and just…wounded in my soul. What about *me?* It seems like the price I paid was so high. *Too* high. When do *I* get to win?"

Craig looked directly at me, his eyes filled with sorrow and empathy. "Oh, sweetheart, I thought you understood," he said softly, tenderly. "You never get to 'win' in those kinds of situations. You just do the right thing, pay the price, and generally no one but you and God knows about it. And that, sweetheart, is what my job is like. Over and over again, that's what I do."

I was nearly overwhelmed with the intensity of my feelings, for I now understood fully what Craig had been experiencing. I knew firsthand the courage that it took to fight for a cause you believed in: I had experienced the frustration and anger that accompanied the act, and I felt the utter depletion and loneliness of doing it in a vacuum that no one but God knew about. I could feel Craig's pain as if his struggles had happened to me because, in an equal sense, they had.

Snuggling up to Craig in the recliner, I wept. There's an indescribable closeness that comes from sharing the same feelings, so deeply, at the same moment. Out of pain, intensity, vulnerability, and risk came the sweet aroma of intimacy.

Moving to a New Location

No matter if you're moving across town, to another state, or outside the country, it's tough. Ken and Jamey just completed a major move to another state due to Ken's acceptance into graduate school. This thoroughly life-changing experience, leaving their extended families and their former careers behind, affected them deeply. "We grew spiritually as a couple through this move," they say, "for we had to depend more on each other in an unknown setting and totally trust God through our transition." As a result, Jamey says, "I've learned through Ken's example and attitude to trust God at a deeper level—to realize His control over our lives."

If a new location meant one adjustment only, it might not be so tough. But unfortunately, nearly every aspect of our lives gets shifted, redirected, and just plain shoved out of whack when we move. The positive part? Those are the times when we have incredible potential to lean on each other in deeper ways, find renewed strength in our bond, and most important, know God in a more trusting way.

If you're anticipating a move, are in the midst of one, or have already resettled, here are some questions to work through:

- Through this process, what have you learned about where you base your security?
- How do you attempt to change those insights into a deeper security in God alone?
- In what area—home, job, routines, finances, relationships— do you feel most insecure as you transition? What elicits the deepest emotions, and what are those feelings?
- What specific change are you the happiest about? The most resentful?
- What are you learning individually about your dependence on God as you go through this time? What are you learning as a couple?
- Sometimes we act out our insecurities in ways that are seemingly detached from the transition itself. (I, Carolyn, have demonstrated a tendency to be overly protective of my time with Craig. I find myself being much less patient about his need to attend evening meetings.) Do you see this in your life—maybe by noting varying insecurities in relation to your job, children, relationships (with your spouse and with others), belongings, and/or finances?
- What was the greatest positive surprise to you about this move? Are there principles here that you can apply to future relocations?

- What was the most discouraging part? How are you dealing with those emotions?

Most might claim there are few positive benefits in the upheaval of moving. It's exhausting not only physically but also emotionally. But Jamey puts her finger right on the spiritual-growth possibilities when she says, "We were taken out of our comfortable lifestyle—basically stripped of everything we were used to except each other...and God!" Like the process or not, being in that position—just the two of you depending upon God—is the best place to be.

Children

When we were expecting our first child and receiving all kinds of parenting advice, a friend shared this bit of wisdom: Parenting doesn't get any better; it just gets *different*. Has that ever proven true! No matter what ages our children are, they still occupy that special place in our hearts that moves us to the deepest levels of joy—*and* pain.

The responsibility of parenting can challenge our faith like no other experience. John and Laura probably express every Christian parent's heart when they say, "Raising three children has certainly caused us to know why we believe—not just that we believe. We've had to explain why certain things are right or wrong and that yes, there are absolute wrongs and absolute truths."

I (Carolyn) remember when one of our sons was on his own, independent and proud of that. But when he hit up against a devastating disappointment, there was nothing I could do except pray and cry with him over the phone. Since he was miles away, I couldn't look him in the eyes and comfort him with my love and acceptance, cook him a special meal, or give him a reassuring hug—all the things moms long to do when a child (no matter what age) is hurting.

As I walked and prayed that morning, pleading for God's healing of my son's spirit, I was suddenly shocked to uncover this hidden selfishness: *I didn't want my son to hurt anymore so I wouldn't hurt.* And then the ultimate sacrifice immediately came to mind—the Father who intentionally sent his Son to hurt to the point of death, taking upon himself the weight of the sins of the entire world. "How could you do that, Lord?" I asked. "How could you endure the pain of sending your Son, knowing that he would die that horrible death?" In contrast to his sacrifice as parent, I was overwhelmed with the shallowness of my seeking to avoid pain.

That Saturday I shared with Craig what I'd learned during my prayer time. We discussed the conviction of my selfishness, the role of pain in our lives—and in our dear son's—and God's example to us as our parent. We pondered and examined whether attempting to shield our children from pain—or subtly conveying to them that we don't want to feel pain with them—may have detrimental effects as God uses difficult situations in their lives to mature, teach, and refine. When we ended our time together, we prayed for our son. We were still hurting with and for him, but we found a measure of peace as we once again gave him to God.

When discussing your children during your intentional time to talk, you might succumb to the temptation to drift to the nuts and bolts of child rearing: what they did this week, what activities are coming up next week, or how they're doing in school. But always try to go one step deeper. For example, if you're discussing your child's gifts and talents, move to character qualities, asking, *How do I envision his using those qualities and gifts for God as an adult? How can we specifically encourage her to develop ways to serve God faithfully?*

That's the key when you discuss your children in an in-depth way: Go behind the questions to your emotions. Then have the courage to take the next step and ask, *What are my feelings saying about me—and about God?*

Here are some additional questions to deepen your conversations about your children:

- What messages do you most want him or her to hear from you?
- How did you fail this week as a parent? Do you need to do something to make that right? Do you need to ask forgiveness? And lastly, do you need to forgive yourself?
- What can you learn from those failures?
- How were you successful this week as a parent? What can you learn from that?
- In what ways might you be attempting to protect your child when you shouldn't? How might God be working in his or her life—ways you shouldn't interfere with?
- In what specific ways is your child challenging you to grow spiritually? What do you think God is trying to teach you?
- What consequences do you need to allow your child to feel right now? When do you interfere? When do you not? And how can you determine the difference?
- Where should you let go? Where should you continue to control? What does each of those look like?

Pam told us that Dwayne has taught her more about God "through his example than anything. He told me when our children were born that it would be his lifelong intention for them to always feel unconditionally loved, to feel and experience God's love through the love of their dad. Though they might sense his displeasure at their actions, they would never question whether he loved them. To my knowledge, they never have."

Still need a discussion question for your time to talk? Then how about this one: How will you fulfill a commitment like Dwayne's in the lives of your children?

Health, Illness, and Injury

You never know what challenge life might bring tomorrow—a diagnosis of cancer; the devastating news that "no, you're still not pregnant";

a tragic accident involving you or your child; or the strain of chronic illness. Any of those can throw you into turmoil in your inner soul, causing a crisis of faith and trust in God. But remember the need to separate *emotions* from *decisions*. Facing surgery, you may feel frightened, insecure, and wary of the future. But you can decide to *trust* God in the midst of all those conflicting emotions. Giving yourself and your spouse permission to feel *whatever* can become the catalyst for the first healing to take place: the healing of the emotional and spiritual life within.

Many couples have suffered the piercing and seemingly endless pain of infertility or miscarriage. Those crises reach far deeper than the physical aspects, for they reside deep in the emotional lives of those who bear those wounds. Don and Rebecca shared that their greatest crisis came when they had a miscarriage. "We were both emotionally and spiritually hurting. Yet we were able to totally rely on God during that time when we didn't understand why it happened." As they look back on that incredibly painful time, they share, "We grew spiritually because we had to rely on God for understanding and comfort."

No matter what physical issues you're facing now, your greatest challenges may reside in digging out the emotions that are hidden deep within. Do you have the courage to unearth and face those? Can you share them with your spouse? And can you lovingly accept each other's feelings, no matter how unspiritual they may appear or how insecure listening to those might make *you* feel?

Here are some questions to guide your conversation:

- What physical issues are you struggling with right now?
- What emotions are connected to those? What feelings are submerged beneath those feelings?
- What fears do you have about the future in regard to your physical struggles? Can you be absolutely honest about them?
- What do your emotions reveal about your understanding

of God's character? Can your feelings help you uncover any misconceptions you might have about God?

- What red-light feelings do you have and what do you think those are saying? (Remember, red-light feelings are those that make you feel uncomfortable; they would include feelings such as anger, sadness, insecurity, and fear.)
- What green-light feelings do you have? What do those say? (Green-light feelings make you feel comfortable; they would include happiness, peace, and security.)
- Are you angry with God? If so, how can you process those feelings with your spouse's help?

TWENTY QUESTIONS

In the early years of our marriage, Carolyn used an obvious signal when she was not particularly happy with me: the silent treatment. That was the only obvious part of this process, however, for when I'd ask her what was wrong, she'd give me the standard reply: *"Nothing."* Then we'd proceed to play the game I eventually named "Twenty Questions."

My part in the game was to quiz her with questions such as "Did I do something? What was it? What can I do to make it right? Are you hurt or angry?" Depending on (1) my perseverance, (2) her stubbornness, (3) the depth of her emotions, and (4) my patience with the game, we might find the questions led to progress in finding the core issue— or simply added yet another problem!

Thankfully, we eventually learned how to work through our problems in a more constructive way. For her part, Carolyn learned to be an active and willing participant rather than resist solving the problem. A major part of her more active approach involved a change that I had to make, however: I needed to allow her to process her feelings *thoroughly* instead of jumping to fix the problem before she was ready to make that step. (For those of you who share my need-to-problem-solve-*now* personality, we'll discuss this more in chapter 12!) We also found that tackling this type of issue was generally a Saturday morning endeavor rather than something to be done on an evening when we were both already tired. And lastly, there were the times when even Carolyn didn't have a clue what the problem was. She wasn't attempting to be resistant, coy, or stubborn. Somehow, a buildup of hurt feelings had collected, totally concealing the core issue. Once again, the detective work would begin!

I (Craig) remember one night when we were racing out the door to go to church. Though we needed to drive separate cars because I had a late meeting, Carolyn still emphatically insisted that we drive two cars but together. That struck me as a bit unnecessary and strange, but I simply replied "Sure," gave her a quick kiss, and proceeded out the door. (Note: Never dismiss those kinds of signals, guys. Trust me on this one.)

As usual, I climbed into my car, fastened my seat belt, and pulled out of my parking space before Carolyn had even settled into the front seat. (What does she *do* in that space of time?) As I headed down the street, I glanced back once or twice. Carolyn was a good distance behind me, but I could see her quite well in my rearview mirror.

When I pulled into a parking space at church, I waited there a moment so we could walk into church together. I even remember thinking to myself how patient and considerate I was being, thinking that must be what she was intent upon and what was so important to her. But then she parked her car, and I saw her indignant expression.

"I thought we were going to drive in together!" she snapped. "Couldn't you have waited for me? You were a good two blocks ahead the entire time!"

I was absolutely flabbergasted. "Carolyn, what on earth? I could see you in my rearview mirror nearly the entire time!"

"In your *rearview mirror?* That doesn't count for being *together!*"

I confess; I couldn't help it. The total ridiculousness of the situation made me laugh out loud! And even though Carolyn was hurt in some way, she also had to laugh. But certainly all that emotion was a signal that something was bothering her, and this scenario was definitely *not* about driving to church!

Sometimes the issues that we've needed to work through on a Saturday have been very intense ones due to the fact that one of us felt deep hurt or anger. (Please note also that there have been times that we didn't wait until Saturday for resolution. If an issue is major enough, that calls for immediate resolution. But fortunately, we both recognized instantly that this wasn't one of those times.) Before heading into church, we quickly discussed the fact that, though she was hurting, her emotions were not at critical stage. We agreed that this could wait until the weekend.

I don't recall the exact questions I asked that Saturday to uncover the hidden issue. But through the years there have been many other times when we've had to use questions to peel back layers to find the core issue. Please note also that those "layers" can be *subconsciously* applied (as they were in this case with Carolyn) when busy schedules force incidents to be passed over, when the actual feeling of deep emotions are delayed, and when others might minimize our intense feelings.

Those layers can be put on through a *conscious* act also: when we stuff feelings, when we decide to deny their existence, and when we intentionally withhold them to "protect" our privacy or our feelings. Needless to say, processing neither conscious nor subconscious layers is easy, but the spouse who decides to intentionally cling to those layers can make the work much more difficult.

Try these general questions to help you tackle those concealed problems:

- When did you first notice that your red-light feelings might have begun?
- What exactly was the incident? What feelings did you feel then? Go beyond the surface feelings: What was underneath it all?
- What other events over the past week(s) prompted similar feelings?
- Can you find a connection between all of these? What ties these together, linking them in your emotional well-being?
- If we divide our emotional needs into four categories—love, belonging, self-worth, and autonomy—which one of these seems to be affected by your feelings? What seems to be your greatest need right now?

Once we settled down with our mugs of coffee the following Saturday morning, it didn't take us long to discover the problem: a series of hurtful incidents—slights from me—had built up and left Carolyn with a deep need to feel cherished. By her own admission, none of those events had been major: forgetting to help with her coat in front of our sons, not holding her hand while at the store, and failing to acknowledge her when she walked into a meeting I was leading. Though these were not significant incidents in themselves, the accumulated effect was still such that it did make an impact on her spirit. She was feeling hurt, even though she had no idea why.

I need to point out that this "hidden buildup" is not confined to one gender or to those with a particular emotional makeup. Both of us have experienced this "layering effect." Over time the collected emotions build into a much bigger issue. We've learned to take note of the buildup signals: Carolyn's signal is usually the outward signs of feeling hurt (minor irritations become major as she then withdraws, "protects" herself by becoming silent or she might even react with anger—merely a cover-up for pain), while mine is often a grumpy or agitated demeanor (my defensiveness and need to protect myself means I often go on the attack very quickly).

....

Can either of you recall a time when the "layering effect" happened in your marriage? Recall how you handled the problem then. How would you handle it differently now? Is that issue resolved, or do you need to still work to get to the core problem and then make changes?

....

Paying attention to Carolyn's signals, patiently doing the detective work, and allowing her to thoroughly process her emotions were all important steps toward healing our relationship. But there's one more dynamic that we needed to implement to keep this problem from continuing: I agreed to concentrate on helping Carolyn feel cherished. Small acts of consideration and care *do* make a difference. (So did the flowers that I brought home the next day.)

And finally, as Carolyn laughingly pointed out, "Cherishing is *not* watching me in your rearview mirror!"

the source of our empowerment

How Do Our Individual Devotional Lives Impact Us as a Couple?

ave you ever heard a piano that hasn't been tuned for years? Certainly every church camp has at least one tucked into a lodge somewhere. Varnish long worn off, ivories chipped, and several keys sticking, that piano can massacre music! Since every key is noticeably bad, however, the sound of one probably doesn't stick out more than another. But on a recently tuned piano—maybe a baby grand at a music hall—a single key would be obvious if that were the only one out of sync.

We can apply this same analogy to our marriages: If we're "in tune," we'll notice immediately when one key is off. Constant tuning through consistent and intentional in-depth communication keeps us aware, alert, and mindful of the off-key notes in each other's lives. The Master Tuner, Jesus Christ, is *the* source of the "music"—the notes used to compose our lives as individuals and as couples. Our job is to stay in tune with the Master *and* with each other.

Probably no other passage of Scripture quite sums up the word *source* as completely as John 1:1-2: "In the beginning was the Word, and the Word was with God, and the Word was God. He was with God in the beginning." Just as our Lord is creator, sustainer, and eternal life-giver of the world, our marriages mirror the same pattern:

- *God is the creator of the covenant of marriage.* As the first created human community mentioned in the Bible, marriage was ordained and blessed by him. Consider the significance of God's choosing to give marriage first-place priority.

- *God is the sustainer of our marriages.* Without his strength and guidance, we would flounder and fail. He cares about the crises and day-to-day stresses we face, providing an undergirding that is *always* available to us.

- *God is the life of our marriages.* It all begins here, in him. In our individual lives and our couple relationship, God supplies the answer to all of our greatest needs—hope, trust, faith, and love.

God is indeed an active participant in our marriages, but to simply rest lethargically in that without doing our part is irresponsible. We dare not be complacent in our efforts, naive in our trust, or less than pro-active in our contributions to the health of our marriages. Have you heard the expression that the greatness of a team is built upon the strength of its individual members? Or that a chain can only be as strong as its weakest link? Though one expression is stated in the posi-tive and the other negative, both sayings drive to the heart of the issue: The overall strength of a marriage is built upon the strengths of the indi-vidual spouses. Ultimately, *I must take responsibility for my marriage and its continued growth.*

Obviously, we're not referring to physical strength. And none of us can claim that we've "arrived," reaching the point of maturity where no more growth is necessary. Instead, we're talking about husbands and wives who are diligently seeking their own individual, intimate rela-tionships with God, committing to that in systematic ways that fit their unique needs and lifestyles. If we agree that our very life is found in God, then we need to be regularly drinking and eating from that source.

Craig and I have always been determined to put a high priority on our individual devotional lives. During many periods, those times have been consistent, encouraging, and relatively calm; we've experienced steady growth that we were eager to share with each other. However, there have also been many times when we've struggled. During those periods our individual devotional times may have slowed, stagnated, or been incredibly laborious. I've told Craig that sometimes it feels like I'm *slogging* through my times with God. I picture myself in hip boots, wading through mud.

••

How do you feel when you consider that God is so actively involved in *your* marriage? Does it motivate you to put great energy into this relationship that he has created, blessed, and given to you?

••

Though Craig and I have never set up a structured system for accountability, each of us senses quickly when the other has been either neglecting spiritual disciplines or is floundering through a tough phase. The outward signs can be anything from heightened insecurity to a short temper. My "hip boot" stage generally produces a mild form of depression. But whatever the outward signs that reveal that one of us is struggling, we don't hesitate to ask, "How are you, really? What's going on? Are you journaling? How's your prayer life?" I must admit, I know it's not going to be a relaxed and easy conversation on a Saturday when Craig has to ask me those questions!

I remember one time in particular when we were considering a job change for Craig. While anxiously awaiting a response from the potential employer, I wrote in my journal that I was deeply hurt, worried, despairing, and very weary of the entire process. Reading through Zechariah for my personal devotions, I had come to chapter 9 on the very day when we expected to receive some sort of definitive word.

Eagerly I claimed the phrase "I announce that I will restore twice as much to you" (verse 12); I took that as a positive sign that God was about to relieve our distress (emotional and financial) and send us on our way to this new and exciting opportunity.

A resounding no came that very evening. And I was devastated.

A fog of deep disappointment settled over my spirit, but in addition, I brooded over the incredible injustice of this experience. Craig had been eliminated as a possible candidate on technicalities. And they were so unfair! How could we have done everything right and still be punished? I blamed the system, yes. But mostly I blamed God. Our battle was about to begin.

Wrestling with God

Have you ever heard that those who frustrate or anger us probably share some of *our* bad habits or qualities—and that we subconsciously recognize them in that person? I've never particularly liked the patriarch Jacob. He was known as a schemer, a man of tricks and deceit, one who literally wrestled with God. Now I don't like admitting that Jacob and I are alike. But if there is any truth to my finding similar qualities in both of us, that evening the wrestling referee could have announced, "Round One!"

Craig and I talked through our anger, disappointment, and hurt, having a long conversation about the truth that God was *not* to blame. Ultimately, we decided that he was much more interested in what this process would teach us about him. And about ourselves. We prayed together, and then, as usual, Craig pretty much went on his merry way, plowing into the week with a renewed spirit. But I was quite a different story. I prayed, continued to study, and begged God to help me let go of this. But the deep hurt continued clinging to my soul like a foggy cloud. Before long, Craig noticed the warning signs that I was slogging through that mud!

By the next Saturday, we obviously needed to tackle this yet again. So when Craig asked, "What's really going on, sweetheart?" I tearfully confessed that I hadn't been able to let go of the hurt, and especially not in the record time in which he had. (It's maddening how quickly he can process those emotions!) Not only did he not condemn me for that, but he then dove to the heart of the problem. "Are you comparing your processing timetable with mine? Because you shouldn't. Just because mine is quicker doesn't mean that it's any more spiritual. We're wired differently, sweetheart. Grant yourself whatever time it takes to heal."

Ever had a "light bulb" experience? A time when you definitively saw God in a new way that illuminated how you viewed yourself? Suddenly I could accept myself in a clearer light: I understood that *God* made me as I am—with deep emotions that take a long while to completely heal— and I should no longer condemn myself for that perceived weakness.

Once again, we took the time to share about the experience and how it had affected us. Maybe I needed one more verbal "cleansing" to release the pain. But most of all, I realized that my energies could be directed toward a process where they would be most effective: accepting myself as I am rather than comparing myself to my husband—and coming away feeling guilty and frustrated on top of everything else! The first true steps of healing had begun.

I also told Craig about my devotions in Zechariah and the resulting disappointment from that. We discussed the need to handle God's Word carefully, and that promises made to the nation of Israel are not necessarily promises for us today. Understanding which ones apply to us and which do not comes under the category of good hermeneutics— which essentially means that we must understand the Bible's construction well enough to apply it correctly to today's situations. If you need help learning how to study and apply the truths of the Bible, we recommend *How to Read the Bible Book by Book,* by Gordon F. Fee and Douglas Stuart (Zondervan, 2002). It's incredibly important to maintain strong individual devotional lives in our marriages. Study that is based on a true understanding of the Bible is *equally* essential.

As I reflect on that time, I realize I wouldn't have grown in the same way through this experience entirely on my own. It took our separate devotional times, our trust in each other, and honest discussion and communication with Craig for God to teach me. Much of my spiritual growth occurred because of our efforts to grow as a couple.

Though I would still need more time to heal during the coming months, I found that I could return to my personal devotional life with a renewed sense of discovery and appreciation for the richness of the book of Zechariah. In my journal, I noted the cleansing fountain of chapter 13, verse 1. Praising God for the symbolic fountain, Jesus Christ, I eagerly wrote out a promise that I knew I *could* claim from chapter 14, verse 1: "A day of the LORD is coming." Even today, I reread and rejoice in the timeless prayer I scrawled that day, "Hallelujah! Come quickly, Lord! Amen."

EMBRACING THE PROCESS

Going to the Source is always going to involve a *process*. We make progress, stumble, take a few steps backward, learn from our mistakes, and then continue on the pathway of growth until we come to yet another stumbling time! As we slowly grow in spiritual maturity, we then have the opportunity to let what we've learned flow into and impact our couple time. A deep and enriching individual time with God can be an incredible resource to enhance our marriages. But first, we must seek that personal time with God, and then second, we must be at peace with the fact that none of this is going to happen instantly or easily. Spiritual growth—individual and in our marriages—is always a process.

Our Individual Times with God Feed Our Marriages

Even though Carolyn originally misapplied the intent of Zechariah 9:12, that area of discussion gave us tremendous resources to talk about how we view God's promises throughout his Word. We reminded each other that he is a God of integrity, truth, and character, *no matter how we may perceive him during difficult times.* We discussed our gut reaction of blaming God—remember that we create an atmosphere for sharing where emotions can be freely expressed, no matter what they may be— but that God is not to blame for this sin-filled and therefore unjust world. All this discussion came about because of Carolyn's individual devotional life.

I (Craig) also was journaling and struggling through this period; therefore, I brought those thoughts, feelings, and desires to our inten- tional—and certainly intense!—Saturday mornings after this incident. The point is this: By going to the Source individually, we empowered our relationship during a painful experience, which ultimately helped us grow as a couple. An incident that could have potentially torn us apart instead became a means by which our relationship became more intimate.

Vulnerability—Before God and with Each Other— Is an Essential Tool for Intimate Communication

If Carolyn hadn't admitted that she was blaming God for her pain, then she would have missed out on the opportunity to grow in her relation- ship with him. Although we tend to conceal these things, thinking it wrong to admit such feelings, hiding that would have been like a cancer deep within. The truth is that hiding her blame of God would have hin- dered her intimacy with him. By also sharing that with me, we both benefited and grew from the resulting in-depth communication.

Note again that *sharing our feelings* is different from *the theology of God:*

Separating "I feel" from "I know this to be true about God" is a distinct and two-step process. For example, I may admit to feeling very angry with God for my child's physical suffering. At the same time, correct theology informs me that God is not cruel but loving. In this way I can openly process my feelings while I separate "how I feel" from "I know this is true about God." We release our feelings for cleansing and healing before moving on to declare what we *know* God's Word says about his character.

Having the Courage to Go a Step Deeper Brings
Us Closer to God—and to Each Other

Once again, we remind you of an incredible opportunity: Will you courageously look at your deepest emotions to unearth what is happening within? What do your feelings reveal about your deepest held beliefs of God? Carolyn admitted to blaming God, but then she went a step deeper by recognizing the guilt she felt for not processing her emotions quickly. That discovery led to even more discussions about accepting ourselves as God made us. If we don't, we tread into the dangerous territory of comparing ourselves to others. And that, unfortunately, only leads to more pain and lower self-esteem. There is only one person who God designed as our example: Jesus Christ, the Source.

• •

Are there areas or issues in your life that need the healing of going a step deeper? What's holding you back? Are you afraid of God's rejection? Your spouse's? Can you go beyond your fears to accept God's love—and that of your spouse?

• •

Couples we interviewed expressed many of the same experiences. Dean and Carol told us they actively seek accountability by "watching each other emotionally day to day to make sure everything is okay." Probably without even realizing it, these two are using their emotions as red- and green-light signals of what's happening underneath! Karl and Sharon told us, "We both are on the lookout for each other and areas of stagnation. We spend time together, enjoy each other, and thus know each other well. This opens the door to accountability." And finally, Pam says, "I can think of times when Dwayne was growing and I wasn't and we both knew it. I felt compelled to get back on track simply because I knew he needed more from me as a wife than that."

STEPS TO SHARED GROWTH

Within those comments are five invaluable hidden steps, so let's back up and pull out each of those.

1. Both Husband and Wife Demonstrate a Strong Commitment to Their Individual Devotional Lives

Allen and Eileen state, "We both agree that before growth can happen as a couple, it must happen as individuals. So we both know it is our responsibility to read and pray on a regular basis." They're absolutely right. Once again, we won't have the depth of riches to give each other if we're not individually going to the Source.

2. The Couple Communicates Deeply Enough to Notice When One of Them Is "Off"

Remember the analogy of the out-of-tune piano? Couples like Steve and Elizabeth demonstrate this "tuning" when they share that they "hold each other accountable with regular times of 'checking up.'" Their choice of words points to yet another application: Doctors tell us that regular checkups alert them to subtle changes that could signal potential health problems. If we're disciplined enough to practice this for our physical health, shouldn't we do the same for the health of our marriage?

3. They Are Proactive: They Watch Out
for Each Other and Share Vulnerably

Trent and Ginger put it this way: "We care enough to stay in tune." And sometimes before one has to point out his or her suspicions to the other, Allen and Eileen admit, "We do share with each other when we haven't been growing individually." That may be a painfully honest confession, but it might also be the first step to proactively reverse the negative slide. By letting my partner know of my struggle, I'm setting up the first line of defense against a possible deeper slide into sin.

4. When Necessary, Spouses Trust Each Other
Enough to Confront

Allen and Eileen agree, "We have accountability for growing individually by noting when something seems out of balance. Discussion then takes place and we'll confront each other." Spouses who have the courage to confront do so with a secure foundation of love and trust. But they also need to approach each other with caution, ever cognizant of the appropriate time and place. (We'll discuss this delicate process more in chapter 11.)

5. Ultimately, the Couple Focus on Their Unity in God

Note once again Pam's motivation to invest in her individual spiritual growth: "I knew he needed more from me as a wife than that—I felt compelled to get back on track." That statement shows a profound understanding of the core issue of a couple's spiritual growth: *We depend upon and benefit from each other's intimate relationship with God.*

If I'm growing spiritually, then I can feed my spouse, which in turn helps him grow and give back to me. Throughout this entire cyclic process, the marriage is growing stronger too.

I go to God where I am fed.
I take that "resource" to my spouse.

We then grow as a couple.

Easy and simple formula, right? Guaranteed to work exactly that way, all the time? Not quite, for God rarely designs simple formulas. His design for spiritual growth in marriage is a bit more complex. The steps get a little more fuzzy when you look closely at the miracle of two people becoming one flesh.

••

Are you having quality times of relationship with God? Are you praying, studying, and seeking him? If not, then can you commit and motivate yourself to do so, not out of a sense of guilt, but because you're missing out on an incredible opportunity to feed yourself and your spouse? If you are enjoying a deep relationship with God, are you intimately sharing that with your spouse?

••

MELDING THE SPHERES

Remember the analogy of the two spheres that we used in the introduction? Each sphere represents one spouse; within those spheres is all that we are as individuals—our thoughts, feelings, desires, hopes, and need of God. Our goal in marriage is unity and oneness, the overlapping and melding of those two separate spheres.

Please note, however, that we do *not* lose a sense of self, autonomy, or uniqueness in that process; remaining uniquely me within our union is an important part of the miraculous "two becoming one." (If one spouse does lose a sense of selfhood, that is not intimacy; that is a description of one partner absorbing the other into his or her personality.) Instead, we are seeking true intimacy and spiritual growth, a miraculous joining that then flows toward a shared relationship with God.

Those who study marriage have attempted to find analogies or symbols that capture the heart of this process. There's the triangle, which pictures the couple moving ever closer to God while moving closer together; circles that overlap and invite God into the bond of that joining; and our own imagery of the spheres. But any symbol pales in comparison to the actual process. To attempt to succinctly picture spiritual growth—or the spiritual growth of a married couple—is to attempt the impossible.

••

Take this opportunity to work through the five steps discussed earlier in this chapter:

1. **Are you both demonstrating a strong commitment to individual devotional lives?**
2. **Are you communicating deeply enough to notice when one of you is "off"?**
3. **Are you proactive? Do you watch out for each other? Are you able and willing to share vulnerably?**
4. **Do you trust each other enough to confront?**
5. **Do you focus on your unity in God? What specifically does that look like in your marriage?**

••

We've already talked about the pattern of each spouse growing individually and then bringing that resource to their couple relationship in an intentional way. But the pattern can also be reversed: What we learn from each other can then be taken back to our individual times with God. Marriage often proves to be the "laboratory testing" of God's character qualities. As Rick says of Tracy (and this was echoed by numerous other couples), "She has helped me to understand God's true meaning of love in that she loves unconditionally." When concepts like unconditional love are then fed back into our personal times with God, the lines of distinction are no longer clearly defined. Each connection with God, whether individual or shared with your spouse, feeds and fuels the other in a mysterious and miraculous way—just as God intended.

This parallel principle—that my individual intimacy with God mirrors my intimacy with my spouse, and that my intimacy with my spouse mirrors my individual intimacy with God—is part of God's incredible design for marriage. No wonder the one eternal symbol for marriage is the ring. What else could capture the endless circle that marital intimacy moves upon?

Conversely, if the cycle is broken—if one spouse does not continually seek a consistent, growing relationship with God—then the circle of one feeding and fueling the other is also broken. In God's grand design, the mirroring of one building up and teaching the other is to be continuous. And looking back to those tried and true analogies, when one link in the chain becomes weak, the entire chain weakens. When a single member of a team loses strength, the team itself loses strength.

Remember then: *Go to the Source.* God is waiting and willing to grant faith, hope, trust, and love in endless supply. We couldn't state it any better than Rick and Tracy so eloquently share: "We both discovered that God was our only strength and driving force for a future together."

How strong is *your* chain?

CHAPTER 7

the true act of submission

Can We Make This Work in Our Marriage?

hen Christians line up on opposite sides of an issue related to marriage, it's usually over the S-word. No, not sin or sex. (But we caught your attention there, didn't we?!) If there's one marriage topic that generates more heated opinions than any other, it's the biblical meaning of submission. And the New Testament passage that receives the most attention in these debates is Ephesians 5:21-33:

> Submit to one another out of reverence for Christ.
>
> Wives, submit to your husbands as to the Lord. For the husband is the head of the wife as Christ is the head of the church, his body, of which he is the Savior. Now as the church submits to Christ, so also wives should submit to their husbands in everything.
>
> Husbands, love your wives, just as Christ loved the church and gave himself up for her to make her holy, cleansing her by the washing with water through the word, and to present her to himself as a radiant church, without stain or wrinkle or any other blemish, but holy and blameless. In this same way, husbands ought to love their wives as their own bodies. He who loves his wife loves himself. After all, no one ever hated his own body, but he feeds and cares for it,

just as Christ does the church—for we are members of his body.
"For this reason a man will leave his father and mother and be
united to his wife, and the two will become one flesh." This is
a profound mystery—but I am talking about Christ and the
church. However, each one of you also must love his wife as he
loves himself, and the wife must respect her husband.

Probably no other passage in Scripture is quoted as often in relation to the sensitive topic of roles for husbands and wives. We can also
probably assume that no other passage has generated as much conflict, confusion, and misunderstanding! But before we enter the fray
and debate the commands and applications, let's look at this entire
portion of Scripture and ask, *What is the logic and tone? What is the
thrust of Paul's theme, which should then direct and guide how we interpret
these roles?*

I (Craig) intentionally began quoting with verse 21, for after many
years of personal study, I believe that is the opening thesis—the topic
sentence, so to speak—for Paul's subsequent discourse. "Submit to one
another out of reverence for Christ" sets the tone for the instructions to
all the pairings he then lists: wives and husbands, children and parents,
slaves and masters. This verse sets a context that totally encompasses and
directs the application. How and why do we submit? *Out of reverence for
Christ.*

First and foremost then, this passage is about modeling our relationships after Christ. We need to interpret the verses that follow in
light of his example, patterning our lives after the way he lived his. So
when we consider Paul's call to submit as Christ did, we must emulate
Jesus' example of submitting to the heavenly Father out of love, first, *for
his Father* and, second, *for us.* That's the same motivation for *our* submission—love for our God and love for our spouse. What exactly did
Christ's act of submission mean? Jesus Christ obeyed his Father and

accomplished his life's calling by doing what needed to be done to save us: He sacrificed his life by dying on the cross.

This call to submission, therefore, means that out of an expression of love, we *voluntarily give up our rights in the interest of serving others sacrificially.* That sets the tone for all that follows; every command to wives, husbands, children, fathers, slaves, and masters must be interpreted in that light. Can you begin to grasp the thrust of this passage from the vantage point of sacrifice? As you read this portion of Scripture, pretend that you're viewing it through a screen that colors and interprets every statement, every command, every emphasis on how we treat one another. For the overriding question in our minds must always be, "What did Paul say about submission through sacrifice now? What does that look like for this specific group?"

••

Have you viewed Ephesians 5 from the sacrificial perspective before? If not, how could doing so change your approach to roles in your marriage? List specific ways that you can sacrificially give to your spouse. What rights, needs, and/or wants do you need to give up as an act of submission?

••

Therefore, as we discuss the first section of Ephesians 5 in which Paul spoke to wives and husbands, we must ask, "What does submission look like for the wife?" And then, "What does it look like for the husband?" (Later the reader must also ask, "What does it look like for children? For parents?" And anyone who thinks that parents don't submit to their children has evidently not yet experienced that blessing. From the first moment that the doctor announces "You're pregnant!" both Mom and Dad are in for a life of sacrificial giving!) In no way did Paul intimate that only the wife submits while the husband does not. The way in which biblical submission works is expressed in differing forms, but each partner is called to a life of sacrificial giving in marriage.

This passage's primary thrust is *not* about structure and authority; instructions for one to rule while the other obeys; or the "chain of command" in the home. That is an off-focus approach to a treatise that begins with, "Submit to one another out of reverence for Christ." Too many husbands—and I (Craig) must admit to having done this in the past—have twisted and corrupted Paul's words, using them as verbal clubs to assert authority in the home as the "head." The tone and attitude directed by Paul is the *exact opposite:* We husbands are to be living in humble sacrifice, not in dominating authority.

ROLES AND LEADERSHIP

The couples we interviewed gave incredibly thoughtful answers to questions concerning roles and leadership in the home; it's clear they've grappled with these issues. From their candid responses emerged the following common opinions and practices.

Shared Initiation

Although a vast majority agreed that "the husband is the head of the home and should be the spiritual leader," in practice, couples indicated that they trade responsibilities in this area. Leading and initiating ends up being a shared role.

Candy says that "Sean is to be the leader and initiator," but they both admit that "either of us can or will initiate a discussion or idea. [Guiding and directing] is shared; we really don't have any hard and fast rules about that. The discussion usually directs the route we take." Although Karl believes that "the husband is accountable for the couple's spiritual growth before God, and Sharon has a great role of encouraging and promoting the process," they both admit that "[leading] is a mutual thing. [Initiating] is also mutual; sometimes Sharon initiates our times together and sometimes I do."

The Reality of Roles

Just as confusion reigns when considering what couple devotions should look like, husbands and wives are also perplexed about their roles in relation to spiritual growth.

Who's responsible for what? If the husband is ultimately responsible for the family's spiritual growth, what does that mean in practical terms? Because of the commonly held interpretation of what couple devotions should look like, Veronica has accepted that "[The wife] should let her husband know that she is willing to study and pray together. It is his responsibility to initiate such times." Then she vulnerably shares, "If I have initiated spiritual things, it has seemed to backfire on us. I think it's a matter of my husband's confidence level in that area. Evan has to be ready to take the lead."

••

In your opinion, what is your role as husband in relation to your spiritual growth as a couple? What is your role as the wife? Do either of you disagree with the other's views? Have you both taken this responsibility seriously enough? Have you learned to be flexible and adaptable?

••

If we have viewed the false ideal of couple devotions as the only acceptable pattern for a couple's shared spiritual growth, then we can understand why many husbands might be threatened by feeling that they must always be in charge, must always initiate, and must shoulder the entire responsibility for the spiritual welfare of their families. It's no wonder they shy away from leadership in this area. The pressure from those unrealistic expectations must be tremendous, as evidenced by their confessions of guilt quoted in previous chapters.

However, if we can view spiritual growth opportunities as times of intentional, in-depth communication, then hopefully *both* husbands and wives can be freed to initiate and guide as the Holy Spirit leads rather than through guilt, unrealistic expectations, and muzzling presuppositions. Some couples appear to have made peace with this issue. Steve and Elizabeth state simply, "Our times together are shared in every way: leading, initiating, guiding, and directing. The role of the husband is to encourage and facilitate times of spiritual direction and formation, and the role of the wife is exactly the same."

Much more often, though, we see ambivalence, probably based upon what couples perceive as *what should be* as opposed to *what is.* This produced conflicting statements among the spouses we interviewed. Molly states, "I think Peter should be the leader in our spiritual growth as a couple." But then she also admits, "I guess I generally take the lead in our actual devotions together." Gerald candidly shares, "I personally always thought it was my role to get and keep the family in church and studying, but truthfully, it has been Merry who keeps us there. Now, after thirty-three years of marriage, we shift roles often about many subjects, including spiritual leadership." What a refreshingly honest note that surely rings true!

Being Responsible for My Own Personal Growth

A majority of the couples we interviewed also stated that first and foremost, the responsibility of the husband is to his own spiritual growth, while the wife is responsible for her own growth as well.

Daryl stressed that "the husband's role begins with his own relationship with the Lord. He must first ensure that he is prayerfully and obediently following God. Then the husband should encourage his wife in her own personal relationship. I must also be open and willing to communicate with Kim, in-depth."

Allen agrees: "I must first be responsible for my own spiritual growth. Then, as I grow in the Lord, I should be steadfast in my convictions, in accordance with the Scriptures. I can then provide a framework for our growth." Eileen continues by saying, "In like manner, I am to be responsible for my spiritual growth first. Then I feel my role is to be a stronghold for my husband, a resting place, a place of peace." They add that "each is then accountable to one another."

And finally, Dwight and Sally echo nearly the same words: "The husband should look after his spiritual growth. Then he needs to be open to times of discussion, being accountable to his wife." They also believe that "the wife should nurture her own spiritual growth, having then the same openness and accountability."

Making Growth a Priority

Every couple we interviewed takes seriously the responsibility of growing spiritually—both individually and as a couple.

Daryl's touching love for God and his wife are palpable when he shares, "I am to love Kim as Christ loved the church. The responsibility associated with that statement is tumultuous." Rebecca believes that "Don is ultimately responsible for the spiritual atmosphere and well-being of the family." However, she also takes a large measure of the weight when she adds, "Don is the indicator of the spiritual 'thermometer,' but I tend to be the spiritual 'barometer.' I generally can sense if things are not right with our 'spiritual family health.'" Obviously, both Rebecca and Don have made their spiritual growth a high priority, nurturing and watching over that process just as they would their children.

Some couples have given great thought to their roles, and their insight is invaluable. Dwayne sees his role as "one of being open to discussion and offering insight. Being able to discuss what God is doing in my life and listen to how he is working in Pam's life is significant." Pam adds, "I believe Dwayne has a serious responsibility before God to be the spiritual leader of our family, to see that ours is a marriage that honors God. I think his role is to care very much about what God is teaching me and the direction our spiritual lives are going." As for the wife's role, Pam sees herself as "being spiritually challenging to Dwayne. I should bring insights of my own to our marriage rather than rely on him to 'teach.' My growth should challenge and enhance his." That's the "mirroring effect" mentioned in chapter 6 in action.

Remaining Flexible

As they pursue spiritual growth, time and lessons learned together have taught these couples to be flexible and to adapt.

Gerald and Merry note that "whoever has an idea or a pressing question gets the ball rolling. This is not a husband/wife role thing. Instead, it's guided by personality, and a proclivity to read and challenge and question." Rick and Tracy have found that flexibility is definitely key: "We share the guiding and directing of our times together. Neither of us has an outline. We just let it flow and see what happens. Sometimes this has been the most interesting and surprising route to take!"

SUBMISSION AND DECISION-MAKING

Submission might come easily when a husband and wife are in agreement, but think about what it takes to submit when you're on opposite sides of the ring! I (Carolyn) must admit that the idea of submitting doesn't sit well with me. First of all, I am very strong-willed, maybe even to the point of being rather stubborn now and then. (But please don't quote me on that. Especially to Craig.) And second, my past connotations with the phrase "submit to your husband" are pretty skewed: being forced to do the very thing I am opposed to, domination by his authority, and an expectation that I'll be asked to demonstrate such a meek and mild attitude that my personality and spirit are destroyed. All done—spiritually?—in the name of "God's will." Since Craig readily admits that my personality and spirit (or "fire" he might say with a chuckle) are what initially attracted him to me, then you can see why we've both struggled with this concept through the years.

However, there is a vast difference between having another person's will *forced* upon me and my decision to *voluntarily* submit my rights, needs, and wants in sacrificial love and service to my God—and to Craig. If Craig comes to me with a spirit of domination, asserting his authority as head of the home, I will most definitely struggle with my attitude, will, and actions. But when he instead demonstrates sacrificial love, I am awed by his heart and love for God in such a way that I cannot help but be moved to respond in kind. Once again, the mirroring of spiritual growth flows back and forth from one to the other. Which one submitted first? Is that even relevant? For the end result—both of us submitting to *God's will*—is the desire of our hearts.

We could debate the terms, definitions, and specific applications in the Ephesians 5 passage, but Craig and I will leave that to other scholars. Instead, we judge that we can best illustrate submission in marriage by sharing a time when we had to make a major decision—when we were *not* in agreement. Since many Christians would argue that, in a situation like this, one must "win" and the other "lose"—that is, the wife should submit to her husband's will—then you might think this story and its outcome pretty predictable. After all, Craig is the head of our home. And I am told to submit to him. End of story, right?

For some time, we had both been sensing that it was time to move on from our then-current position. We looked at a few job offers and turned them down. Others turned *us* down. But one day Craig received an offer that he was very excited about. After longing to return to Colorado for years, he heard the mountains calling! With an enthusiastic twinkle in his eyes and eager optimism in his voice, he listed off all the "wonderful opportunities" and "amazing advantages" of this position. For all those pluses, however, there was only one major drawback: I did *not* want to do this. Not one bit.

At the time, I was frightened by how much we were "not on the same page." We'd had several job offers, changes, and moves in the past. Generally, we were both pretty much in agreement about all of those. So it was unusual for us to respond with such vastly different opinions. Where Craig saw positives, I could find only negatives. When we agreed to write out lists to pray over, he wrote as pros those things that I listed as cons. My minuses column was incredibly long, while his was amazingly short. No matter how we looked at the issue, we couldn't come together. There was no middle ground, no compromising. Either we took the position or we didn't, and that meant that one of us had to change his—or her—mind.

••

Can you think of the last time you needed to make a major decision and you were not in agreement? How did you go about resolving the issue? Were there areas where you submitted yourself to God and your spouse in the process? Or can you now see ways that you should have sacrificed your rights? How can you use this process in the future? What decisions are you facing right now?

••

Many couples might assume that the course of action at this point would be clear: Craig's role as head of the home should prevail and I would submit. After all, isn't that what Ephesians 5:23 indicates? Many would say Craig should have asserted his authority, forced the decision upon me, and carted one unhappy camper across the country.

But that's definitely *not* the way Craig views his headship—nor is that a picture of the submission that we see portrayed in Ephesians 5.

Instead, he led by example, exhibiting a godly and genuine willingness to voluntarily give up his rights, wants, and needs through sacrificial giving to me. He granted me the freedom to earnestly seek God's will by stating that, unless we *both* could agree to take the position, then we judged God was either saying "no" or "wait—until both of you *are* in full agreement."

We decided to do what we'd done years ago when faced with another major dilemma. Each of us would earnestly ask God, "Please change my mind, if that's what you desire. Mold me to your will, whatever that may be." I said earlier that Craig's genuinely sacrificial response to our differences gave me the freedom to seek God's will. But I also fully realized the tremendous trust he'd placed in me—in my intimate relationship with God (and my ability to know and then accept God's will) and for our future. That lent an urgency to my prayers that was indescribable.

I remember many agonizing days of prayer, journaling, studying Scripture, and feeling confused, isolated, and simply miserable! One day I lay prostrate on the floor, begging God to change my mind and my heart, if that were his desire. During this time, Craig also continually sought God's will for us, asking God to change *his* mind if that was, indeed, what he wanted. On Saturdays, we'd talk and question and vent (mostly me!) as needed. As I struggled and wrestled with my God, Craig remained loving, supportive, and patient. Though his opinion never changed—and I am convinced that he would have changed his opinion had God directed him to do so—he demonstrated unwavering commitment to our process. It's one of the greatest gifts he's ever given me.

Finally, I felt my mind, will, and attitude begin to settle and ease into...surrender? I don't know if that is the most accurate description of what took place, but I do know the wrestling stopped and I was at peace within once again. I knew without a doubt that we were to accept this position based upon two beliefs: First, God had impressed this upon my heart as his will for us. And second, I decided to trust in my husband's godly character and his decision-making process.

So we did indeed travel across the country to those glorious mountains. And there God did an amazing thing, something that filled us both with awe at his grace and goodness. Within a year of moving to Colorado, God called Craig to become president of Denver Seminary, a step that was obviously in his plans for us throughout that agonizing time of discerning his will.

If I had not submitted—if we both had not submitted as we judge God asked us to—would we be in this position now? I don't know, and that speculation is wasted time and effort. But Craig and I firmly believe this: God ultimately cares more about the process than the decision itself. Learning to *live* in sacrificial love is a far greater task than saying yes or no to an opportunity. And discerning his will—being conformed to him in what we think, what we value, and how we act—is the ultimate journey in this world.

HUSBANDS: LIVING SACRIFICIALLY OR IN AUTHORITY?

I (Craig) imagine that the great debate over exactly what "headship" means will continue until Christ returns! Until that time, it's my desire as a husband to *serve* as the head and lead my family—not by ruling with authority but instead by being the first to give sacrificially to my wife and to our life as a couple (see Ephesians 5:25). I realize the need to continually submit my "rights" for the sake of serving, and I pray for the grace and wisdom to do just that.

Guys, that's an imposing task. But before we can even begin to strive for that goal, we need to ask ourselves, *What does living in sacrifice look like as opposed to living in authority?* Here are some pictures of what it is…and is not.

Living in Sacrifice Is Not a Feeling. It's a Decision.

I certainly don't *feel* loving toward Carolyn every day, but I can and must *decide* to love her. Scripture states very succinctly, "This is love for God: to obey his commands" (1 John 5:3).

Living in Sacrifice Is Not Mere Words and Empty Promises. It's Doing.

Over twenty years ago, I could have *promised* Carolyn that we would communicate more. I could have merely *offered* to share my feelings, be vulnerable, and seek in-depth intimacy. I could have *guaranteed* more time talking together as we snatched conversations in the car, on evenings when I was tired, and in between discussions with our sons. Instead, I gave her a weekly time of intentional conversation. In my eyes, sacrifice looks like Saturday mornings. (I'm not implying that I don't look forward to our Saturday mornings; instead, I'm emphasizing that I committed to them—and intend to keep that commitment to Carolyn.)

• •

To the husband: In what ways do you need to give up your rights and sacrificially give to your wife? What decisions do you need to make to carry out a commitment to her? Specifically, how can you nourish her? cherish her?

• •

Do I have the right to golf on Saturday mornings? Absolutely. Do I have the desire to sometimes withhold difficult feelings—the times I feel insecure or rejected or petty? Often. Do I sometimes feel a desire to abandon responsibility and *just once* do whatever *I* want to do? Oh yes. But living in sacrifice means that I attempt to live as Christ did, obeying, submitting, giving.

Living in Sacrifice Is More Than Providing.
It Means That I Nourish My Wife.

Let me state this clearly: Ultimately, our needs can *only* be met in God. Jesus Christ is the only one who can fulfill our deepest needs in every way. But within marriage, God provided the means for us to give to each other like no other relationship. Carolyn depends upon me to nourish her. (In Ephesians 5:29, the *New American Standard Bible* uses the word *nourishes* rather than *feeds,* as it is rendered in the *New International Version.*) Since Ephesians 5:29 admonishes me to do that as I would my own body…and "just as Christ does the church," then the emphasis moves from job and paycheck to the nourishment and feeding of my wife's soul and spirit.

Living in Sacrifice Is More Than Care.
It Means That I Cherish Her.

Once again, I prefer the *New American Standard Bible's* choice of words in verse 29: *cherishes* as opposed to *cares for.* Cherishing Carolyn is a sacred trust and opportunity on my part. When I show my wife that I cherish her, I announce clearly, "You are the delight of my life." (If you have questions concerning exactly how to cherish your wife, we'll cover that in more detail in chapter 8.)

Living in Sacrifice Is Loving. As Christ Loved
the Church. As I Love Myself.

Nowhere in the fifth chapter of Ephesians do I read that husbands are to "rule" or "have authority over" or "dominate" in the home. Instead, I find the words *love* (mentioned seven times), *give up, nourish, cherish,* and *be united to,* which challenge me to live as a godly husband according to those guidelines. It would be much easier to rule, assert my authority, and force my will. It would be easier, but isn't that really the coward's path? God's call to a lifetime of sacrifice is *not* the easy journey. And it's not what this world views as just or fair.

It's just the journey God asks us to take.

Wives: Living Sacrificially or in Subservience?

Wives, we're also called to live in sacrifice, and our part is no less daunting or demanding. Our battles include attitude (as in rotten?!), submission to the point of subservience (which is *not* what God asks), and the challenge of integrating a sacrificial spirit with strong personality. Once again, the best model of negotiating that tricky balance? Jesus Christ. Let's take a look at some guidelines that will help us emulate him.

Living in Sacrifice Is Not a Feeling. It's a Decision.

Remember our story earlier in this chapter about the job change? I (Carolyn) submitted to God first and then to Craig, agreeing to take the position in Colorado. There was one important part that I neglected to tell you until now: My underlying feelings were *not* in line with the peace that I felt about my decision. On the contrary, I felt insecure, wary, and disappointed. Nor did those feelings change during the move or for some time afterward. But once again, there is often a great gap between *what we feel* and *what we do* when the right path is clear.

Living in Sacrifice Is Not Mere Words and Empty Promises. It's Doing.

Passive aggression. I have no idea who first coined that phrase, but that level of stubbornness sometimes fits me like a tailored suit. Perhaps you've heard the illustration about the little boy who was forced to sit but then belligerently declared, "I may be sitting down on the outside, but I'm standing up on the inside!" That's often me! So I must quickly make this addendum to our story. I was *not* a model of sweetness throughout our decision time, nor was I beyond being grumpy—and taking that out on Craig.

Are you familiar with Paul's vulnerable admission of his struggles in Romans 7:15? He admits, "I do not understand what I do. For what I want to do I do not do, but what I hate I do." I can sure relate! The point seems to be that we must make the decision to do what is right, and then we'll need to make it again and again and again. Especially those of us with personalities more susceptible to passive-aggressive "standing up" while "sitting down"!

Living in Sacrifice Is More Than Token Respect. It Means That I Show Respect by Valuing My Husband.

As we read Ephesians 5, Craig and I wonder if Paul was partially targeting deep needs that were affected by the Fall. When Adam and Eve sinned, they covered themselves, hiding from a vulnerability and intimacy that once came naturally. Because of their sin, they used barriers to hide from each other. Was Paul addressing the barriers that we continue to use today, ones that further complicate and cover the needs that possibly were met before the Fall?

When Paul commanded husbands to love, nourish, and cherish their wives, he drove to the heart of what I need most from Craig. Craig tells me that deep respect for him—who and what he is, his vocation and his decisions—all go to the core of what he needs from me: to be valued as a man and husband. In the story I told earlier, I decided we should accept the position in Colorado because I judged it was God's will for us; I also trusted Craig's decision-making process. Thus, my submitting to him by valuing his opinion, wisdom, and godliness was a validation of Craig himself.

Living in Sacrifice Is Submission. But It Is Not Subservience.

In Luke 9:23, Jesus told the disciples, "If anyone would come after me, he must deny himself and take up his cross daily and follow me."

Certainly that's a clear picture of the submission we've been talking about—denying myself to follow Jesus. But that invitation from Christ assumes the decision to follow is a complete abandonment and denial of myself, a 180-degree turn to him. That assumes that *I have a self to deny.*

If we have little or no self-esteem to begin with; if we are so subservient that there really is no "cost" to the decision; and if we see no worth in our own opinions, thoughts, and feelings; then our submitting is little more than slipping into an easier pattern. It is only when we find worth in who and what we are before God and then truly give that back to God—and then to our husbands—that we have actually denied self and sacrificed *something.*

Once again the model that Christ set is ever before us. Remember his agony in the garden? He admitted freely and honestly his desire to not go to the cross. But then he submitted to his Father, saying, "Your will be done!" The pattern Christ demonstrated is to honestly admit to God and to ourselves our opinions, thoughts, and feelings. Only then do we truly submit when we give them to him, for *that is a gift of truth and reality.* That is a gift of *me.*

· ·

What do you need to change in your life to free you to live in sacrifice? What do you need to give to your spouse? What must you both do to invest in your relationship and make it a model of Christ's sacrificial giving?

· ·

To husbands: If you have insisted on getting your way as the authoritative head of the home, then you have denied your wife the opportunity to give herself to God—or to you. Instead, can you reform your role to model Christ? To *serve* as head, by sacrificially giving to her?

To wives: If you have been so subservient that you have not known and accepted your worth to God before you submit, then you have denied yourself the opportunity to really give yourself to God—or to your husband. Can you now accept your value before Christ and present him with a true gift?

If you find that these dynamics have been true in your relationship and you are determined to change, then the ramifications may be overwhelming in their scope. We suggest that you seek help from a counselor to guide you through this delicate and courageous process.

developing and encouraging each other

How Can I "Invest" in My Spouse?

everal years ago, Craig and I had just started out on a two-hour trip when he began excitedly telling me about a book he was reading. We always look forward to talking in the car, so he chatted away about how interesting the book's concepts were. However, he took great exception to one chapter in which the wife of the author had asked her husband something to this effect: "Why is it always about *you?*" Craig explained what she'd meant by her question—that their lives and decisions and focus centered around the husband. She judged herself peripheral and, sometimes, a mere "accessory" to *his* life. Craig was firmly convinced that I would never ask him a question even remotely resembling that.

I allowed a few moments of silence and took a deep breath, knowing that we were about to plow into a murky marshland of our own. And then I quietly but firmly said, "Often I feel exactly the same way." The relaxed and easy atmosphere quickly turned intense and emotional as we debated that topic for the next 120-plus miles!

Needless to say, our views concerning this issue were greatly polarized. I judged that since Craig has always been our primary breadwinner, his job directed most of the major decisions in our lives. *His* career controlled where we lived. *His* future needs for advancement required sacrifices for further education. And by the very nature of the positions that he'd held (professor or pastor), *his* job regulated what our lifestyles would look like. My logical, reality-accepting side understood that Craig's being the primary breadwinner made all of those necessary. However, my emotional side did not accept that we were a functioning *team* in every way. For many deep-seated reasons (which I'll dig into a bit later), I felt resentful and hurt at the same time. It was as though Craig were standing at the whirling center of a vortex, and my needs, desires, and wants were merely swirling around the periphery.

Having brought up the book only because I (Craig) was convinced this would be a positive conversation, I couldn't have been more flabbergasted by Carolyn's response. Rather than the expected affirmation for my role in our marriage, I felt attacked! Therefore, I shifted into defensive mode. I told Carolyn that I viewed her input, career, and activities on the same level as mine. I saw us as equal partners in every way. When she then accused me of having a "Priority Number One" schedule, I peppered her with examples of times when *her* needs or wants had indeed come first.

However, no matter who was right (it was wasted time and effort to continue down that track!), the important fact remained that our *perceptions* were different. If we as husbands and wives both believe that our opposing views are true and absolute fact, then *Houston, we have a problem!* On that long (oh, was it long!) trip, I eventually came to the conclusion that I needed to listen to Carolyn's heart, patiently pulling out the deep-seated emotions and unmet needs that made those perceptions real for her. Real for our marriage. And because of that, I had the responsibility to not only listen but to then seek compromises and workable solutions to begin fixing what she saw as broken.

Men, hear this: The fact that I perceived our dilemma quite differently was *irrelevant*. When barriers like these are revealed, our combined energies—both husband and wife—must be directed toward healing the breach between us. Since Carolyn viewed this as a hurtful wound, my job was to move from "defending my position" to "fighting *for* us." (Note that Carolyn needed to do this also.) Though these next several pages will be directed by Carolyn toward wives, it is equally important, men, for you to listen—to really *hear* what is being said. There just may be wounds in your relationship that you need to recognize and respond to appropriately.

Also, your situation may be entirely different: You may both have full-time jobs outside the home, or one of you may be a stay-at-home parent—mom *or* dad. Possibly the wife is the primary breadwinner in your marriage. However you share the need to provide and care for your family, these issues will be relevant, since they float to every situation. All of us tenuously juggle the demands and stresses of relationship in the midst of those pressures.

Helping Your Spouse Develop as a Person

As Craig and I attempted to break down those barriers and discover the core issues, we found this to be a complicated issue. But we began with the presupposition that Craig's actions toward me specifically need to demonstrate: *I am interested in helping you, my wife, develop fully as a person. Your contributions, evidenced by the gifts God has given you, are of equal importance to mine. Therefore, I will invest in you.* These principles hold true in our marriage and in every marriage in which a husband seeks to help his wife develop fully as a person.

Speaking as a wife, I judge Craig can exhibit that to me by:

At Key Times, Sacrificing His Rights, Needs, and Wants for Me

Several years ago, I (Carolyn) took a research course toward a master's degree. I needed an entire day each week to make the commute, attend class, and study in the library on campus. Since our sons were in elementary school, that meant a major sacrifice of Craig's time to pick them up at school, come home at that hour, fix dinner, and then be Mr. Mom for the evening through homework and bedtime routines. He not only did that willingly and without complaint, but his excitement about my class was a tremendous encouragement.

••

Can you think of times when your spouse has already made sacrifices for you to achieve a desire? Are there other areas where he or she might sacrificially give to help you achieve some goals? What workable, intentional, and step-by-step plan could set that into motion?

••

In so many ways, we both benefited from what I learned. Our friends Sean and Candy have had that same experience, stating, "We share how the individual activities, classes, reading material, or conversations affected us. When the previously mentioned activities provide meaningful thoughts or suggestions, we try to share them for application in both our lives. So, in a sense, we're taking one class as an individual, but getting the notes for two!"

Craig's enthusiastic support for my taking that class was a key event, one that would set a pattern for future activities requiring his active sacrifice: He encouraged me to finish writing a novel that I had not yet sold; by providing time, he made it possible for me to meet the deadline for a nonfiction book; and he helped our family establish Tuesdays as my day to write, when he would be responsible for dinner for all of us. (The pizza delivery guys soon knew us on a first-name basis, however.)

Seeking Ways to Help Me Feel Cherished

Craig is the only man who should make me feel cherished. That is his role alone, which makes this a privilege and challenge at the same time! When I do feel cherished by him, I know a surge of joy that is beyond description. But when it's lacking—and painfully so, as described in chapter 5—then we're caught up in unmet expectations (probably hidden ones that I haven't verbalized), hurt feelings, and misunderstandings.

To keep that from happening, we need to describe what cherishing looks like. First of all, it's a statement, action, or nuance that announces, "Carolyn has a special place in my heart that no other woman holds." Sometimes this can happen between just the two of us, when no one else is present. At other times, I need for Craig to make this clear precisely because others *are* around. And a third situation may occur when we're in a crowd—but the wink or special look passing between the two of us shuts out the rest of the world! In any of those situations, however, the act of cherishing is directly connected to our intimacy and the bonds of marriage. Craig's attentiveness to this evidences our affection and tenderness, his commitment to our covenant, and the unique and special relationship we share.

• •

Do either of you have a deep need to be cherished? What specific actions can your spouse take to help you feel this way? An assignment: Sit down together and discuss this need and how you both can make this happen.

• •

Even if we understand generically what cherishing is, however, we can still suffer hurt feelings because of hidden expectations and unspoken hopes. I eventually came to the realization that I had no right to expect Craig to help me feel cherished if I hadn't given him clear suggestions on how to make that possible. Therefore, after years of trial and error, missed opportunities, and eventual success, we discovered that these occasions are (still!) excellent opportunities for him to help me feel cherished:

Acknowledging My Presence

When I walk into a room—and especially when there's a crowd present and Craig is already there—his intentional eye contact, smile, and wink announce "I *noticed* that you've arrived. And I'm glad you're here!" It's such a simple thing, but it can make my heart swell with joy.

Protection

In a throng of people, on a busy street, in a darkened alley, or anywhere that I might feel vulnerable, I love it when Craig takes my hand. His intentional concern for my safety and his efforts to make sure that we won't be separated are subtle actions that make me feel secure.

Public Appreciation

This opportunity doesn't happen often. But when it does, I glow in the praise of his sincere and genuine words.

Praise in the Presence of Our Children

Only Craig has the opportunity to build up my image in this unique way before our sons. Comments like "Your mom is incredibly special" and "I think your mom is the most beautiful woman in the world!" leave lasting impressions concerning me *and* the institution of marriage in our sons' hearts and minds. An added benefit: He's modeling for them how to be loving and thoughtful husbands as well.

Surprise Notes, Cards, Small Gifts

When Craig gives me a totally unexpected note or small gift (anything from a card, flowers, or a CD), his gesture states, "In the hustle-bustle of a normal week, I was thinking about you." That effort suddenly makes a small note of great worth.

Journaling When We're Apart

Over the years, Craig has taken several long trips without me to another part of the world. I dreaded the time of separation, but his homecoming was always especially sweet because he wrote a daily journal to me while we were apart. Those notebooks—which chronicled his feelings, experiences in detail (which he would have forgotten otherwise), and how another culture looked through his eyes—are priceless treasures. (I also journal to Craig during those times.)

Surprise Trips

Craig has arranged—totally on his own and unbeknownst to me—several wonderful trips. We've journeyed to New York City for the delights of Broadway, Chicago to see *Les Misérables,* Cancun, and several one-day trips that were just as meaningful to me—because Craig planned them and therefore said to me: *I want to be with you. And I will go to this much effort to show you my love!*

Viewing the Things That Help Me As Also Beneficial to You

Craig learned that I had a passion to write and that I desperately needed that outlet for creative expression. I feel fulfilled, productive, and happier when I'm working on a project. There is a noted difference in the atmosphere around our home when I'm writing!

> What creative outlet needs do each of you have? Are they being fulfilled in some way? No matter what stage of life you are in, you must still have at least one activity that helps you grow as a person. Can you identify one that you could do with your spouse's sacrificial help?

Also, I have more to bring to our marriage when I'm in the process of researching, discovering, and creating: I have more to talk about, I can share what I've learned, and I judge that Craig grows because of the resources I have to offer him.

Attempting to Enter My World

One of the agreements resulting from our discussion that day in the car was that Craig would read one book of solely *my* choice every year. Since I enjoy fiction—while he reads only nonfiction—my choice for him would most likely be a novel that made an impact on me. Let me make the ramifications of Craig's sacrifice clear: He would never *choose* to read a novel. Wading through fiction is as unwelcome as a root canal, in his opinion. (He just recently experienced that too.) And Craig has virtually no spare time. Therefore, that gift to me—attempting to share in the emotions I felt from a moving story—is priceless.

For those of you in marriages with stay-at-home moms of young children, we have a major challenge: Why not have dad take on this role—for a day, several days, even a week? We think his appreciation for all the things that moms of preschoolers do would increase profoundly after an intense few days of "initiation"!

• •
How can your spouse enter your world? Can you agree upon one or two specific, workable suggestions? How do you think you will feel if he or she follows through?
• •

No matter whether you have a full-time career, work part-time, are a stay-at-home mom, or work out of a home office as I do, this challenge can be met if you both seek creative solutions. Communication, compromise, and commitment are all necessary parts to this process.

Telling Me Through Words and Actions That You Need Me

Delving into the question, "Why is it always about *you?*" was a major turning point in our marriage, for it pushed us to look deeper at some nagging issues. While I accused Craig of being the central focus of all we did together, he was sincerely perplexed and confused by my charges. "You say we're a team," he said, "but I'm at the center? Where exactly is the breakdown?" His very real bewilderment and concern became the motivation for me to step back, release my prickly defenses, and begin to look deeply within. I realized that Craig was a very definite part of the workable solution—*but so was I.*

For his part, we discussed, negotiated, and agreed upon two key strategies for implementation: First, Craig would attempt to view my career as equally valid and worthwhile; second, when appropriate and needed, he would fit his world into *my* schedule. The specific ways in which we worked those out called for constant compromises on both our parts, but we have made significant progress toward achieving those goals.

The core issues, as you would expect, were tougher to uncover and resolve; these related to my feelings, deep-seated needs, and subjective perceptions. At the heart of it all, however, I recognized one driving force: *I needed Craig to need me.* Far beyond all the other compromises and agreements, my development and encouragement as a full partner in our marriage hinged on knowing that we were a team in every way—and I held an equally important role. Craig had frequently told me that he needed me in the past, but I simply didn't believe him. In my judgment, there was too much evidence proving otherwise. His independent nature, strong emotional life, and natural capabilities just didn't leave him appearing to be needy, period.

However, a few months after our intense conversation, I began to notice a subtle shift in my perceptions. First of all, the strategies we set before us and Craig's commitment and follow-through on those promises began to make an impact. His attention to my schedule, my career, and my activities spoke louder than mere words. Every time he checked with me before scheduling an evening meeting—rather than simply assuming that date would fit into my calendar—I heard him say: *Your time is important to me. Your needs are equally as important as mine.*

At about that same time, Craig's new administrative assistant made a concerted effort to pass along Craig's complimentary comments about me, knowing that I'd never hear them otherwise. Her intuitive understanding that those anecdotes would give me joy and strengthen our marriage was a timely godsend. Whenever she passed along comments like "Craig proudly told the class that you're the best part of him" and "He shared that he fears two things: being unable to take care of himself in old age...and losing you," my self-esteem grew and I grasped just a bit more that he really did need me.

• •

Is it important to you to believe that your spouse needs you? Do you grasp that as truth or not? Can you list some specific ways to meet the needs of your heart?

• •

Also, all our efforts on Saturday mornings toward true vulnerability—sharing intimate feelings—were finally paying off. No longer did Craig attempt to disguise or hide the emotions that demonstrated his insecurity, rejection, or uncertainty. Instead, he had reached a level of trust in me where his manhood was not threatened by admitting to weaknesses. And when he showed tenderness or wept openly in public, I knew that we both had come a long way in our journey toward a healthy expression of emotions.

Finally, I love how Craig demonstrates his need of me when he asks that I join him ("because I need your help") in so many aspects of his career. Anything from teaching, editing, traveling, and discussing strategy to simply being by his side as we interact with guests on campus all tell me clearly: *We are a team and you are an invaluable part.*

I know we have more years of hard work before us, for this is an issue that will always present challenges. As long as we both have careers—and ones that mean so much to us—we'll face constant stress, compromises, and adjustments when our schedules collide. But I judge that we can much more firmly acknowledge, *Who is it all about?* Jesus Christ. And our desire to further his kingdom as a team.

The Need for an Invitation

As I (Craig) ponder the development and encouragement that Carolyn has invested in me, I want to stress the most important first step that had to be taken: *I had to invite her in.* All too often, we husbands criticize our wives for not being an active part of our interests ("She'd *never* watch a football game with me!"), our emotional lives ("Honestly, she just can't relate to what I'm experiencing"), or our careers ("How could she understand what the stress is like there?"). My desire is that my life partner and best friend understand *all* of those areas. If I use the excuse that she can't relate—or I don't have the courage to share my emotional life—then we will remain separate, alone. As husbands, our attitudes, sincere invitations, and the opening and offering of our hearts all set the stage for how our wives are able to respond to us through their emotions, their intellect, and their actions.

We don't want to be sexist in assigning those particular roles, however, for your situation may be reversed. In your marriage it may be the wife who needs to invite in her husband. But no matter which of you is less emotionally demonstrative, which one moves too quickly toward *fixing problems* while exhibiting impatience with *expressing feelings,* or is less verbally expressive overall, *that* person needs to take the initiative and do the intentional work of inviting.

The same needs listed by Carolyn (to husbands) apply once again. A wife's actions specifically need to demonstrate that *I am interested in helping you, my husband, develop fully as a person. Your contributions, evidenced by the gifts God has given you, are equally as important as mine. Therefore, I will invest in you.*

As a husband, I judge Carolyn can best demonstrate that to me by:

Joining Me in Interests That We Can Mutually Enjoy

When we first got married, Carolyn was definitely not athletic; she would be the first to admit that. I remember attending a college class when a professor used the illustration that *everyone* knows how to ride a bike. I was sitting in the front row, shaking my head and smiling sheepishly when the professor glanced my way. "Um, not my wife!" I admitted, and we all chuckled. Though Carolyn was a bit chagrined when she heard the story, she still didn't learn to ride a bike for several more years, after our second son was born. But that was all it took: After acquiring that skill, she quickly added one athletic challenge after another in an attempt to keep up with the three of us boys and our perpetual motion!

....

Can you think of some interests that the two of you can enjoy together? How can you help make them enjoyable and beneficial for each other? If one of you has abilities beyond the other (for example, you would normally cruise at a much faster pace on a bike), how can you adapt your exercise and attitude so that he or she does not feel as though you're not enjoying the time together?

....

Although Carolyn merely tolerated playing catcher for our backyard ball games (the family dog was actually better at that position, anyway!), she soon learned to not only be an excellent biker and hiker but to thoroughly enjoy those activities. And now that we're empty nesters, care to guess what we plan for a day off during vacation? A mountain hike or bike ride. It is a good day indeed when I crest a sharp rise, discovering that I'm finally at the top of a challenging trail up a mountain…and glance over to share the fulfilling accomplishment with my best friend.

Carolyn still insists that she should never be described as athletic, though I would disagree with her. But if that is true in any way, then the significant point is this: She cared enough to acquire the skills and personal enjoyment of those physical activities so that she could develop and encourage me and our relationship. The fact that she enthusiastically joins me rather than staying home alone is a tremendous gift. And besides that, it's also great fun!

Using Her Gifts to Show an Interest in My Workplace
My aesthetic abilities are pretty much nonexistent: I absolutely cannot grasp matching colors or patterns in fabrics, arrange pictures on a wall, or place furniture in pleasing ways in a room. When I attempt to sort books and various items on a shelf, you would think a toddler had contributed his expertise. In other words, my decorating talents are about zilch. So when Carolyn offers to make my office comfortable and pleasing to the eye, I am very appreciative of her efforts.

• •

If applicable to your situation, have you invited your spouse into your workplace? Have you sought his or her approval or advice for its efficiency and appeal?

• •

Please know that this is not something that I require of her, nor do I ask her to do this in a condescending way. Instead, this is a gift that she willingly and cheerfully gives to help me accomplish goals at my workplace—a comfortable atmosphere that is efficient, effective, and attractive. Carolyn's touch is apparent and obvious after she's brought order and aesthetic appeal to my office, and I'm convinced we all benefit from the improved environment.

Attempting to Enter My World

Once again, before this can occur I must fully understand these steps: First, I lead the way by inviting Carolyn into my world; second, I must accept and believe that "she *can* relate"; and finally, I must work diligently to make sure these things happen. Talking out loud about my feelings, workplace situations, strategies, goals, and philosophy allows Carolyn to experience my day with me—and to know what questions to ask.

> Do you regularly share your day with your spouse? Are you able to communicate only the situations—or do you include your emotions? Can you agree on guidelines for when (and what) you will and will not share? How can this exercise be beneficial to your relationship? Or maybe you're at the opposite end of the spectrum: Do you have a hard time letting go of work, not being able to talk about anything else? Do you sometimes vent your work-related stress on your family? How can you and your spouse find a compromise in relation to sharing about the events of your days?

However, we are *not* suggesting that you reveal confidences, those situations that would be inappropriate to share with others, or each and every happening from your day. No job—and especially those in counseling, medical, or pastoral areas—allows for that. But revealing your emotions about experiences as opposed to specific situations shapes the core of what she wants and needs to hear from you. Those feelings comprise the gift of your inner self. An added benefit? She'll hopefully understand much better why you came home grumpy, weary, content, or frustrated beyond belief!

Often when I come home after an especially long and stressful day, I want to forget every aspect of it. It's very appealing to simply put my job totally out of mind until I have to deal with it again the next day. I'm especially not eager to revisit the conflictual situations, stressful issues, conversations, or decisions that will throw me right back into the vortex of all those messes! For those occasions, Carolyn and I have a standing agreement: Sometimes I do need a total break, and we agree to process the feelings on the coming Saturday morning. Other times I find that talking through the day with Carolyn actually helps me feel better, view situations from a different perspective, and gain insight from her. Speaking my feelings out loud at those times is therapeutic and healing. However, let me stress again that I still must be intentional and pro-active for that opportunity to occur. My natural instincts and desires would send me immediately to my recliner and a ball game every single evening!

Appreciating What I Need in My Life to Be Healthy

The connection between good health and the habit of processing stress is well documented. Since we all encounter stress to some extent, we must find practical and workable ways to relieve its damaging effects. I've found that I can best dissipate stress through regular exercise; swimming, walking, golfing, hiking, or biking are essential for me to stay physically, emotionally, and spiritually fit. Fortunately, Carolyn understands that need and not only doesn't resent time given to those, but she encourages me to exercise regularly.

At the same time, I am careful to not take advantage of Carolyn's generosity in this area. Whenever possible, we exercise together to enjoy each other's company, and there are certain times that I choose to forego golfing with the guys—Saturday mornings, except on rare occasions, and date nights. With organized planning, a genuine desire to find mutual interests, and a bit of sacrificial giving on both your parts, you can find an exercise program that is healthy and fun.

....

What do you need to do to relieve the stress in your life? How can your spouse support you in practicing these activities? Are you balancing this need with time for each other? Are there any activities that you can enjoy together?

....

When we experienced those first intense emotions of hurt and anger in the car, it would've been much easier to avoid the conflict and tension and simply gloss over the breach that existed between us. We definitely would have had a more pleasant conversation—and a seemingly shorter ride!—had we not cracked open those sensitive areas. But when you're intent upon growing in your relationship, there is often only one way to remain healthy. You look at the raw wounds, experience the pain, and seek healing. The quick fix of avoiding reality only means that the wound is undercover.

Are there areas in your marriage that will take courage to reveal? Take each other's hands, affirm your love for each other, and ask God for the courage to begin.

mostly for men

What Do I Gain by Risking Intimacy?

 real *man's man.*
I guess I don't really understand exactly what that phrase means. I suppose it describes rugged, tough, we-can-handle-anything kind of men. You know the type. As a matter of fact, you might consider yourself to be in that category. It's a funny thing, though. No matter how macho these guys appear, they tend to crumble at the mention of one small word: intimacy.

Recently I observed this phenomenon at a reunion of old friends. The husbands (all of them the man's-man type) were standing in a huddle talking as the wives chatted in another huddle close by. One of the men overheard a woman mention the word *intimacy,* and he immediately blurted out, "Hey, guys, let's get out of here. The ladies are talking about intimacy!" Everyone laughed. But to my amazement, within seconds every one of those guys had left the kitchen to take safe haven in the family room.

Guys, what is it about intimacy that makes our knees tremble and our palms sweat, triggering an intense desire to escape? Frankly, I'm not sure there is only one cause, but rather I tend to think a number of factors are at work. That was certainly the case for me.

One key reason could be that we just don't see the value of attempting to build intimate relationships with our wives. Of course we *say* we do, but do we really believe the effort will benefit us personally?

••

Think about how you react to the word *intimacy.* Does the mere mention make you want to escape? Discuss with your spouse what each of you thinks of when you picture intimacy in a relationship; do you note any misconceptions in your thinking? Can you accept that there is value (for you) in deepening your intimacy with your spouse? How might you benefit personally from making intimacy with your spouse a priority?

••

When Carolyn and I first committed to reserving our Saturday mornings for each other, I privately questioned how valuable these times would be, especially for me. I know that may sound selfish, but I did wonder. (Of course, I didn't say that to Carolyn; I may be dumb at times, but I'm not stupid!) I could see that our Saturday mornings together would probably improve how Carolyn felt about our relationship. However, I couldn't imagine the many valuable improvements that would occur in my relationship with Carolyn, with our two sons, within me, and in my relationship with God.

THE VALUE OF INTIMATE RELATIONSHIPS

For years I thought my role as husband and father was to appear in control and able to fix anything that happened in our family life. Everyone seemed to feel more secure when I projected an attitude of confidence. So when Carolyn and I attempted to have intimate conversations and she shared deep hurts and concerns, I thought my job was to provide solutions. That was something I could do quickly and easily, and it certainly matched how I defined my role as husband and answer man!

As a Husband: No More Answer Man

The problem? Usually Carolyn didn't want solutions; she was capable of developing her own. Before we started our Saturday morning times together, I remember feeling frustrated that she was taking so long to get to the answers that seemed so obvious to me. Many times I stopped listening when Carolyn was telling me about a personal struggle and started forming the perfect solution for her to apply so we could get on with discussing other things!

I remember a week when Carolyn was exceptionally busy. She was overwhelmed with our family's endless to-do list and preparing for upcoming activities that required so much of her. That Saturday morning she started explaining how stressed she felt. Well, when it comes to time management and handling numerous projects at the same time— I'm your man! So what did I do? I immediately began to expound upon some excellent time- and project-management tips. That was exactly what Carolyn did *not* want to hear.

• •

Do you see yourself as a fixer—one who immediately desires to move quickly to solutions? How can you concentrate more on simply listening to your spouse's feelings? List specific ways in which you will both benefit from this exercise of concentrating on listening as opposed to providing solutions. How might this change your view of yourself as well?

• •

The look of disappointment on her face was immediate and clear. Instead of my spouting a list of fascinating and strategic management ideas, she longed for me to listen, show I cared, and affirm my belief and trust in her. Also, she wanted time to explore her feelings verbally and to move to solutions at her own pace, not mine.

Eventually, I came to realize that Carolyn usually didn't want me to say anything in particular—just to listen compassionately and ask the kind of clarifying questions that showed I wanted to understand. She didn't want me to act any particular way, either. Instead, she wanted me to be truly present without "acting" at all. Finally, she didn't want me to fix things—and certainly not her. She wanted me to be myself and honestly admit that I didn't have all the answers.

When I started to replace the role of fixer with the role of listener, I saw a change in Carolyn and in our relationship. As she began to feel trusted and valued, she more freely shared her inner thoughts and feelings with me. Since I no longer felt responsible to fix things, I was able to listen to what she really wanted me to know and understand about her or about a problem we were facing. As I gradually stopped viewing myself as the answer man, I started feeling much more comfortable when we discussed those tough life issues that have no real solutions. We grew closer as a couple because she felt listened to and encouraged. I didn't have to come up with great answers or solutions; I just needed to be there, truly present to receive the gift of her inner person.

As a Dad: Building My Sons' Confidence
Applying the listening concepts that I learned with Carolyn to my relationship with my two adult sons has become invaluable. Instead of falling into the habit of being the answer man, I have learned instead to ask their opinions and help them think through the options to arrive at their own answers. This builds their personal confidence and communicates that I value them as men and trust that they can make wise decisions. After many years of progress, today I can proudly say that I only give the right answers sometimes—but usually at the wrong times!

As Spiritual Leader: Following a Natural Course
Throughout our marriage I have tried to appropriately assume my role as a spiritual leader in our marriage and family. I admit confusion and

failure characterized my thoughts and attempts to provide this leadership. Early in our marriage, I thought I had to initiate all prayer, devotions, and spiritual exercises. I tried the roles of "fix it man," "nothing phases me," and "I can do anything." None of these worked. Frankly, I felt pressured into doing some things that I was uncomfortable attempting.

Yes, being a leader means that you need to lead even when it puts you in an uncomfortable position. Still, I questioned why this role of spiritual leader in the home didn't come more easily. I think it was because I was trying to be something that I wasn't. I had established roles and expectations that I didn't—and couldn't—measure up to. Eventually, the feelings of failure and confusion resulted in my giving up. Have you ever felt the same way?

Through our Saturday morning conversations, I discovered a new role: being who I am as a child of God. Instead of trying to create artificial moments of spiritual leadership, I began to find that God brings natural moments into my marriage and family life that allow me to express and develop my role as spiritual leader.

• •

If you are a parent, how might this change of perspective (less answers from you; more trust put in them) benefit your children? Do you need to listen to their opinions more? allow them to think of solutions on their own? How can you specifically apply these suggestions in your family? Also, in what creative ways can you "lead naturally" in your home?

• •

During our younger son's teen years, we decided that instead of doing devotions and praying together, we would commit to skiing one night a week during the ski season. There was one condition: He had to read a chapter each week from an agreed-upon book, and we would discuss it as we ate dinner, drove to the ski resort, and rode up the lift.

Many times fellow ski-lift passengers looked at us with strange glances as my son and I discussed aspects of our spiritual lives and biblical values.

That was just one example of how I found ways to fulfill my role as spiritual leader. Today both of my sons and I naturally find ways to discuss matters of spiritual significance as we talk over our careers and their decisions as they plan their futures. I encourage you to explore more natural methods of assuming your role as spiritual leader in your marriage and family.

How Intimacy Changed Me

To my amazement, I began to probe into some messy areas of my own personal life and found that sharing them with Carolyn gave me better perspective and strength in dealing with these areas. Because I'd given Carolyn the freedom to explore her thoughts and feelings with me without my trying to fix them, I began to trust her to listen to me as well. This change took courage and hard work. I thought Carolyn would feel insecure if I admitted that I didn't have the ability to fix the impossible. To my surprise, just the opposite was true: She felt more secure when I realistically and honestly admitted my own feelings of insecurity and not having the "right" answers.

....

In the past, have you allowed yourself the freedom to explore your deepest feelings? Discuss this honestly with your spouse. Do you tend to present yourself as always secure and able to fix everything? If so, why do you think you feel a need to do this? What value might you find in admitting your fears and insecurities?

....

Strong personal confidence is helpful to me as a leader. But at times people feel insecure around me because they wonder if I ever struggle or feel afraid. Sharing your own sense of fear with a person who portrays himself as fearless can be intimidating. One day after I shared some personal fears with Carolyn, she surprised me by saying, "I feel more courage to face my own fears when I hear how you work to overcome yours."

Freed from the Bondage of Denial

Who am I as a man? Do I measure up? Many people who minister to men list these as two of the most frequent questions men privately ask themselves. In his book *Wild at Heart*, John Eldredge says it this way: "This is every man's deepest fear: to be exposed, to be found out, to be discovered as an impostor, and not really a man."[1]

....
Have you ever felt the bondage of hiding your true feelings? Share an example of this with your spouse. With your spouse's help, input, and gentle encouragement, discuss why you felt a need to do so...and how you might learn to release yourself from future denial. How might this make you a better leader?
....

This inner, unspoken fear of being found inadequate was a major roadblock to building an intimate relationship with God, Carolyn, my sons, and others. Over time during our Saturday mornings, I found the courage to speak this fear and experienced release from its bondage. Yes, bondage. Hiding from how we feel as men and from our thoughts of how we measure up creates a climate of denial and inauthenticity. We are held hostage by our attempts to pretend in front of others and hide from how we are actually feeling. Internally, this hiding creates a tension that is difficult to explain. You have seen it in others. Clearly, they are

---

1. John Eldredge, *Wild at Heart* (Nashville: Nelson, 2001), 45.

feeling a strong emotion such as fear or hurt, and yet are denying those feelings by trying to act confident and unconcerned about how they are being judged by others.

As a leader I face numerous decisions. Team building and consensus are two important values for me. However, there are times when, as a leader, you must stand alone. In the past, I tried to convince myself that standing alone didn't affect me. Now I know that when I must stand alone, the act of being honest with the right people about how I'm feeling and sharing my doubts about my leadership actually gives me the courage to stand. It is a strange effect, but a freeing one.

After sharing with Carolyn my inner struggle about how I measure up as a man and person, I felt energized and relieved—much like what I feel when taking a fifty-pound backpack off my shoulders during our many hikes in the Rockies. Carolyn's loving affirmation of my manhood and leadership ability provided a newly discovered confidence and source of courage. Why hadn't I released this pressure years earlier? Some inner tension still remains; however, it has released its grip and I feel freer to explore who I am as a man and a leader.

Freed to Be Intuitive

Accepting and learning to appreciate my intuitive side was another personal improvement. I am a very logical person, due to both my personality and my professional training. Hunches are nice, but a truly informed leader doesn't operate on hunches—or so I believed. I have since replaced that notion with a willingness to embrace my intuition. In today's world, leaders are asked to make more and more decisions with less and less information. Many times we have to act on intuition and then look for validation as we move forward. I still work to uncover hard data to validate intuition; however, paying attention to my hunches and proceeding cautiously makes me a better leader.

Recently, I had to make a decision. Our leadership team was split down the middle on which course we should take. I delayed as long as I could as I tried to build consensus. It was time to lead. Certain variables and factors that could inform the decision were missing and impossible to identify. My rational thoughts told me one thing, and my inner spirit said another. Prayerfully, I sought God for the answer to become clear so that the entire team could jointly decide. Yet no clear answer emerged. In the past I would have chosen the rational choice. To my amazement, I chose to act on my intuition.

Are you more logical or intuitive in your decision-making process? What about your spouse? Honestly ask yourself: Do I dismiss my spouse's opinions because of his or her leanings in regard to logic versus intuition? Discuss together: What is the value of each approach? Should one weigh more in importance than the other? How can you bring intuitiveness and logic together in your decision-making process?

The result? Two months later God confirmed that the intuitive choice was correct. Now, this is not always true. The key for me is that in the past, I wouldn't have even considered my inner "gut." But my Saturday morning discussions with Carolyn slowly allowed me to become confident in this side of my personality, and it has made a major difference. I still work hard to verify my intuition, but I am more comfortable pursuing that aspect of my personality.

Carolyn, on the other hand, is truly an intuitive person. She comes to that bias through personality and spiritual giftedness. In our early years of marriage, Carolyn's intuition and my logic collided! Frankly, I tried my best to make her more logical by helping her see the weakness of living her life based on intuition. Over time, I came to realize that I was the deficient one. Maybe I started to accept my intuitive side more by learning to value this part of her personality. By accepting Carolyn just as God designed her and allowing my intuitive side to soften my logical side, I have become a more balanced person and a better leader. Also, Carolyn's thinking seems more logical to me these days—another unexpected value of our Saturday mornings, as she too has learned to appreciate her own ability to think logically.

Freed to Feel Emotions

In his book *Birth of the Chaordic Age,* Dee Hock argues that the most important part of being a leader is the process of self-management.[2] And one key in self-management is becoming aware of your emotions—an insight that should positively impact your role as a leader. As a young man, I generally denied my emotions. My common response to a hurtful or frustrating experience was "That didn't bother me."

However, on Saturday mornings, Carolyn and I talked about experiences from our previous week and began to explore our feelings about them. During our conversations I felt insecure and uneasy. Too many times I found ways to change the subject. Carolyn's encouragement was a key in helping me develop self-awareness of my emotions. Her careful listening, encouraging spirit, nonjudgmental attitude, and good questions helped me to explore my feelings more openly and deeply.

I remember a time when my supervisor instructed me to release a certain employee. While I had major reservations about this decision and asked that we wait, I submitted to his authority and dismissed the employee. Immediately, a loud and intense negative reaction erupted from the rest of the staff, a reaction that I had anticipated. To my surprise, my supervisor publicly announced that I had made the decision unilaterally and that he didn't support my move.

Needless to say, I was outraged, but I quickly moved to hide my

---

2. Dee W. Hock, *Birth of the Chaordic Age* (San Francisco: Berrett-Koehler, 1999), 69.

feelings. When Carolyn and I discussed this situation, I wanted to pretend that I had processed all my emotions and that it was time to move on. Yet Carolyn kindly and persistently kept asking me critical questions. Eventually, I honestly admitted my feelings, talked through them with her, and could finally move on without being overly controlled by these emotions. An added benefit to honestly facing and processing my own feelings was that I could then better confront my supervisor without attacking him.

••

Do you have a tendency to deny the existence of your emotions? Explore reasons why you might feel a need to do this. What benefit can you see to overcoming this tendency? Also, does it take you a period of time to recognize the existence of a feeling in your life? How can your spouse help you reveal those feelings? How might improvement in this area positively impact you?

••

Over time and through many other conversations with Carolyn, I began both to recognize that I did feel strong emotions and to understand more clearly what I was feeling. Through our talks I learned that I tend to discover these inner feelings days after the actual happening. The result? Today, I still need time to discover some of my feelings about a situation. However, I recognize more quickly what I am feeling and better manage my earlier tendency to pretend that all is well when I'm around others. With this new emotional awareness, I can better ensure that my reactions to people and situations reflect what I judge is wise, not some unacknowledged emotions.

Freed to Pursue Greater Intimacy with God

On my spiritual journey with God, I judged that my sense of obedience was well developed. Commitment and dedication characterized my relationship with Christ: I stood ready to give myself for his cause and will. Yet I longed for more—an intimate relationship with him. In the same way that I had presented a confident face to Carolyn and my sons, I came to realize that for years I tried to present a perfect or at least a well-managed face to Christ, also. Inadvertently, this created a barrier to my spiritual growth.

A couple of years after Carolyn and I began our Saturday morning times together, I decided to apply some of the same principles to my time with Christ. Using my newly purchased journal, I started to record my prayers and attempts to honestly communicate my thoughts and feelings with God. Slowly I started to notice a change. A dialogue began as I started listening and hearing God's voice in my life in new ways. I found that when I honestly discussed with Christ all the good and the bad, he met me there. (Don't worry; I'm not suggesting some sort of mystical conversation. There were no audible voices. However, I did find clarity of hearing God's "voice" that I hadn't experienced before.)

• •

Honestly appraise your personal devotional time. Are you able to be completely honest with God in a dialogue with him? How do you (or can you) achieve that goal? As a couple, discuss what an intimate relationship with God looks like. If you do not currently write your prayers, thoughts, and spiritual insights in a journal, would you con-sider adding that discipline to help you seek God more intimately?

• •

This motivated me to seek more time with Christ and to allow the Holy Spirit to probe more deeply into my spirit, revealing the good and also those things that Christ could transform for his glory. Over time, a newly discovered closeness characterized my thoughts and feelings toward God and our relationship. For the first time, I judged that Christ and I truly were on a journey together. Here was yet another value that

I had not anticipated when I agreed to spend my Saturday mornings with Carolyn.

It is amazing what learning to truly listen to someone can do. Through all this improvement as a person, husband, father, and leader, I now so deeply value our Saturday mornings and other times of seeking intimacy with each other. Oh, I still feel uncomfortable at times and wonder what I should do in certain situations. But I am no longer deeply afraid of my intimate moments or conversations.

I struggled over what to say to you men who read this chapter. Have I made the transition sound easy? Certainly, it wasn't for me. Please know that your journey may look different and yet similar to mine. My desire is to help you see the value of pursuing intimacy with your wife and with God and to encourage you to seek the benefits that will come as a result. Adding more guilt feelings would only paralyze you. Instead, seeing the possibilities will motivate you. Begin a journey of discovery and challenge. Becoming the men God means for us to be will bring freedom and contentment.

Starting this week, commit to setting aside regular time with your wife. By pursuing intimacy with your wife, and inviting her to help you explore intimacy with God, you will see God make significant and wonderful changes in your life as a husband, father, leader, and follower of Christ. Go ahead and start this journey with the confidence that God will meet you at each turn.

mostly for women

Why Should I Risk Being Hurt Again?

everal years ago, a friend and I were sharing about our marriages, laughing and teasing about our common misunderstandings as we tried to figure out men...and as they attempted to understand us! It was a lighthearted discussion full of chuckling about the "we're from two different planets" lingo until the conversation took a serious turn.

Suddenly, my friend's eyes filled with tears. "I've given up," she said, her voice breaking with emotion. "If I try to seek intimacy and be vulnerable, I just get hurt. Again. And I can't take that anymore. I'd rather not even try than go through that kind of pain again." My heart ached for her, but I had no solutions. I felt helpless and shallow as I simply expressed how sorry I was and reassured her of my love.

I wish I could now say that I'd be fully prepared to help that dear friend fix her marriage and achieve her heart's desires. Armed with workable answers and guaranteed solutions, I would proceed to list all the ways to make her marriage—and yours—all that it could possibly be: intimate, trusting, growing, faithful, and happy in every way. But Craig and I hope that you understand by now that we're all on a journey—a journey that entails constant effort, struggle, and sometimes two-steps-forward-and-three-steps-back kind of work. It can be discouraging, painful, full of joy, and incredibly frustrating—all in one day. But if there's any one key secret to real progress, it's this: We don't dare give up. *Ever.*

Remember the paradox of never accepting divorce as a possibility, never mentioning the word in jest or anger, and at the same time believing that divorce could indeed happen to any of us? Because of that, Craig and I have agreed to be proactive, doing everything we can to keep our marriage growing and strong. Whenever I've been tempted to give up, keep the hurt feelings to myself, or not risk yet another confrontation on an issue that just won't go away, I remember the paradox of that commitment. When I'm weighing whether I should say something that Craig may not agree with, if I'm debating whether I will once more place my ego and self-esteem out there to possibly be hurt again, or if I'm hesitant to reveal what I'm truthfully feeling, I'm reminded of our agreement. And I ask myself, "What's the greater risk?"

Let me be painfully honest: I'm a coward at heart. So when I'm debating whether to plunge into another sensitive, land mine–filled area, I don't do so easily or without fear. And just as with any other marriage, Craig and I have no guarantees. Every time we open a wound, expose the infection, and begin the work of healing, we take a chance—just as you do. But the possibility of suffering even greater pain, not seeking reality and truth between us, and seeing the hidden barriers grow if they are not addressed are, in my opinion, far greater risks.

What, then, is our greatest enemy? What keeps us from achieving intimacy in our marriages? *Fear.* And that fear takes on many different facades. There's the fear of being controlled. The fear of being negated. The fear of being preached at. And as I've already mentioned, the fear of being vulnerable…and then being rejected. Each one is formidable and capable of obliterating any spiritual growth in your marriage. But I'm convinced that our fears gain and keep control by remaining covert.

They feed off of the subjects that we don't dare openly talk about together. *And that's exactly how they retain their firm hold over us.*

• •

Can you gather the courage to discuss these issues with your spouse? What might hold you back? How can you act with courage— in spite of those fears?

• •

When one of our sons was just a toddler, he took a terrible fall down our basement steps. He thankfully suffered no lasting physical scars, but the traumatic experience left him with a justifiable fear of heights. Therefore, years later when his elementary school teacher announced with great fanfare that the entire class would "ride to the top of a mountain on an incline train!" it was no surprise to us that our son said no. A very resolved and firm *no!*

Craig and I respected his right to have the final say on this issue; at the same time, we knew the ridicule he would face from his fellow students if he didn't go. But more important, we understood that there were lessons for him about facing a major fear, talking through all the possibilities, and helping him see that he could decide *to act* in spite of the reality that *he still felt afraid.* So we placed all those fears out in the open. We dissected them, affirmed the God-given need for fear in our lives, and most of all, reassured him of our love, no matter what decision he might make.

Our son courageously rode up and down that steep mountain, facing his fears literally head-on! The lessons he learned from that day served him time and time again as he grew into manhood.

Now to *your* story. Can you face the fears that may threaten the intimacy of your marriage? This is my hope for you: By honestly revealing your fears and openly discussing them together as husband and wife, you may plow through the first major stumbling block to intimacy. Even that first step will take courage, but know that bravery never takes place in a vacuum. I judge that true courage is facing the obstacles before me *in the midst of my fear.* And just as with our son, don't forget to affirm your love for each other—within the circle of God's love. With his help and guidance, you may find a joy that is far more powerful than the futile forces of hidden fears.

The Fear of Being Controlled

Craig has outstanding debating skills: He thinks well on his feet, processes information at lightning speed, and forms a logical and compelling argument for his beliefs within moments. What does that mean for me? I'm toast. As I've told him, "You can shred me in seconds if you wish!" Therefore, I always tentatively approach conflict with Craig through the grid of the very real knowledge that he has the ability to control our discussion—its progression, direction, components, scale.

. . . .

Do you judge that you've been controlled by your spouse in the past? Can you grasp the difference between his or her controlling your discussion and controlling you? What can you do to prevent the fear of being controlled from happening again? If your spouse does indeed attempt to control you, how will you respond?

. . . .

Controlling our *argument,* however, is vastly different from Craig's controlling *me.* I am the only one who can allow that to happen because, as an autonomous being, I've been empowered with the ability to throw off that victim mentality. (Who empowers us? Jesus Christ, through his gift of salvation and the defeat of sin's power through the Holy Spirit!) Instead, I have the ability, the right, and the power to grasp my personhood and assert, "This is who I am; this is how I feel." No matter where a conflict takes you, no matter who controls it, or who's the most skilled in arguing, *no one* has the right to argue with your feelings. Because they just are. Because they are you. (A quick reminder: We're talking about the *instant* spark of emotions that you feel, not the continuing emotions that you nurse. If you choose to feed and build that red-light emotion, to speak or act in a sinful way, then you have indeed entered the realm of immorality.)

Please know that it took years for those principles to move from my head to my heart, and even longer before I could begin to apply them with my "shredder" husband! If one of you has superior debating skills, then you also will need time, reminders, patience, and continued work to put those principles into practice. Also, how these issues apply to confrontation needs to be discussed at much greater length; therefore, we'll come back to this in more detail in the next chapter on confrontation.

THE FEAR OF BEING NEGATED

After we graduated from college, Craig accepted a position as youth pastor at a church in Ohio. The teens were lovable, fun, and eager to grow, making this a ministry that we both fell in love with quickly. But the negative side was that Craig soon became totally engrossed in this job; there was little room left for me in his world. The void was painful, and I found myself constantly nagging about his lack of attention to me and how he had shut me out of his emotional life. But I had no idea how much more I could hurt until the day I felt simply invisible to him.

Craig was leading a group of teens around the back of the church building to a door that was always kept locked. He charged along—in the lead, as always—the teens following immediately behind; I brought up the rear, lagging behind. I saw Craig open the door with his key, swing it wide, and then disappear into the church. The kids quickly followed, and because I was so far behind, I had to run to catch up at that point. But just as I reached for the door, it swung closed. Clicked soundly. And locked again.

I stood there a few moments thinking, *Surely he'll notice that I'm not with him and the group. Certainly he'll come back, apologize, open the door, and let me in.* So I waited. And waited. Until I realized—tears beginning to sting my eyes—that he hadn't noticed. And he was definitely not coming back to let me in.

I gathered my courage to face the humiliation and then walked around to the front of the church to unlocked doors. Just down the hallway, I discovered Craig in his office with the teens. They were talking and laughing, totally oblivious to the fact that I had been locked out. *All* of them. Including Craig.

When I finally got Craig's attention and said to him, "Hey! I was locked out, and you didn't open the door for me!" his only response was a quickly muttered "Oh, sorry." And then he immediately returned to interacting with the kids. Suddenly, I felt so small that I was nearly invisible, as though I'd been totally negated. And to have that happen in *Craig's* eyes made it one of the most painful times in my life.

I don't know many experiences that are more wounding than feeling negated, as though I simply do not exist. Interact with me, argue with me, even *fight* with me—but above all, please don't treat me as though I'm a void. Being invisible might be a wonderful trait for the Invisible Man, but for a woman in the union of marriage, it can be devastating. When I'm nullified in that way, I'm tempted to judge that I have no value, worth, or contribution to offer us. I assume that we've all experienced this to some degree—at least enough to make us frantic to avoid that possibility ever again.

Any time your feelings are dismissed as trivial, unnecessary, overreactive, unspiritual, or simply not worthy of being heard, then you also may feel negated. Yet once again I urge you to remember that God created you *exactly as you are.* Your deepest emotions are a revelation of the person he created you to be, the person he intimately loves! If you believe that is true, then you have the power to separate out your hurt *feelings* from this *truth: No one* can ever negate what God has designed and made in love.

• •

Have you ever felt negated by your spouse? Explain—in clear but loving detail—how that made you feel. Can you separate your feelings from the truth that God sees you as a person of great worth?

• •

I hope this book has made it clear to you and your husband that feelings reveal the innermost person. That they *just are.* Your sharing them with each other is an invaluable gift of intimacy. Neither of you should ever negate the other's feelings or personhood. But should that happen, remember this: You were created by God. He loves you deeply. And *no one* can negate what the Sovereign God creates and loves.

THE FEAR OF BEING JUDGED

Have you ever summoned your courage to share brutally honest but "unspiritual" thoughts or feelings with your spouse, only to have him turn into a "spiritual sheriff"? Were you judged so quickly—maybe even with an impromptu sermon attached—that you made a mental note never to take that risk again? If so, then you faced yet another facet of rejection, one that possibly crushes your spirit more than any other. This rejection reaches not only to the heart of your relationship with your spouse—but also with your God. When you take a hit in both of those areas, the reality is that your soul suffers a grievous wound.

Why might one of you take on this role of spiritual sheriff? Maybe your spouse is covering his own insecurity or fear of being out of control of the situation. If he's focused on fixing you, he may feel overwhelmed with a problem that is beyond his capabilities. If your husband takes pride in himself as "head of the home," he may feel frightened to realize that he simply cannot fix the issues—nor fix you. It could be that he feels guilty and partly responsible. If so, maybe he's deflecting the blame from *himself* by preaching, teaching, and judging *you.* He may also be deflecting blame because he sees his own weaknesses in your admission, and that is simply too much to bear. Possibly he's frantic for an easy solution: "You and God have to deal with this!"

Some might argue that they would never judge their spouses. But if your husband has ever suggested that your emotions are unspiritual, then he has indeed preached at you. It has just been packaged in a more subtle way. If he has *shamed* you for being vulnerably honest about a desire for material things, for wanting revenge for a deep hurt, for thoughts that escalated to a bitter attitude, then he has judged you. (Keep in mind that these roles could be easily reversed: Are you, the wife, the spiritual sheriff in your marriage?)

••

Do you judge that you've been preached at by your husband? Can you forgive that? How can you approach him about this and give gentle but clear suggestions on how he might change? Also, have *you* ever been guilty of preaching? If so, you need to ask for forgiveness, both God's and your husband's.

••

Once again, you're faced with the dilemma: Will you take the risk of being judged again? Armed with the knowledge that honesty and vulnerability are two of the building blocks of intimacy, you must weigh the cost of the risk versus your silence. By approaching your discussion with the guidelines for feelings (review these in chapter 3, if necessary) and a clear statement of "I know these attitudes and desires are not spiritual, but I need to be brutally honest with you in the interest of our relationship," then you may find that your in-depth communication brings a surprising reward: the ability to then be brutally honest with your God. And find there forgiveness, healing, and deep change.

THE FEAR OF BEING REJECTED

Intimacy, by its very nature, requires that we place ourselves in a vulnerable position: at risk of being hurt. By revealing our innermost emotions, desires, and needs, we essentially say: "Here. This is my ego in the palm of your hand. Take it and do as you wish." If that tender offering has ever been rejected in the past—through a demand for justification ("*Why* would you feel that way?"); by negation ("You *really don't* feel that way"); or with disapproval ("You *shouldn't* feel that way")—then the still-raw wound or sensitive scar becomes a stark and blaring reminder: *Don't go there again. You could be hurt! The risk is far too great.*

••

Do you have the courage to be vulnerable and risk being hurt yet again? If you are hesitating, then your first step is to ask God for the desire and courage to attempt this. How specifically will you approach your spouse? No matter what happens, remember above all how much God loves you, his child.

••

Those inner voices are correct: It's a very real possibility that you could be hurt again. But the opposite is also equally true: You could reach a level of intimacy that is beyond words and touches inexpressible joy.

when confrontation is necessary

How Do We Cut to the Core Issues and Find Healing?

ou can sense the tension growing all week, bubbling like water in a pot when someone turns up the burner on a stove. Eventually, it will work its way up to a full, raging boil. Then one of you—maybe both?—will explode like a mass of pasta and water overflowing the pot and creating one huge mess. Except that pasta and water can be cleaned up much easier than the consequences of a major confrontation between husband and wife!

Sometimes when something has been simmering in our relationship, Craig and I find that we need to address the problem immediately. At those times the issue is so potentially divisive and dangerous to our marriage that it warrants carving out time to talk—*now*. Usually, that happens when one of us has hurt the other deeply. That may have occurred intentionally or by accident, but either way, the remedy is the same. We work on us immediately.

At other times, we're quite aware that the simmering has begun, yet we agree that tackling the issues can and should wait until our Saturday morning time together. The decision to delay talking usually occurs during a hectic week—when we're out in the evenings or too emotion-ally and physically beat to tackle the problem when we *are* home. In the past, when we've attempted to fix the issue during hectic weeks, we usu-ally discovered that we merely applied a short-lived solution: The core problem remained untouched and merely circled right back. Jim and Renee made the same discovery, saying, "We must commit to unrushed time to work things through; if we try to fix things too quickly, it only leads to a blowup later!"

Timing is significant: It takes honest and direct communication to decide *when* you need to confront the problem that lies between you. All these factors must be taken into account:

- How deeply are one or both of you hurting? How angry are you? (Please note, however, that anger is rarely the core feeling; usually, it's peripheral to hurt, rejection, fear, and so on.) Imagine yourself putting this off for a few days. Is that possible for you, or do you judge that this must be tackled immediately?

- Evaluate the incidents that prompted your hurt or anger: Do they hint at a major core problem or a passing frustration?

- Are there circumstances during the week that will prohibit your having the time and energy to tackle this? Do you have evening meetings or appointments that cannot be postponed or com-pany staying in your home? Are your weekdays so stressed and busy that you haven't sufficient energy for the evenings?

- Can you both agree that this problem can wait for resolu-tion during your scheduled time to talk? If not, as soon as possible, you must find the time and energy for the sake of your relationship.

It's important that neither of you merely acquiesces or feels pushed aside if you elect to wait to tackle those problems. If either of those occur, then you've only added another layer of hurt to the original mess!

When It's Time to Confront

When we have one of *those* Saturday mornings, my (Carolyn's) heart is usually in my throat and my stomach is in a knot! After more than twenty-eight years of marriage and the inevitable conflict that comes from living together, it's still never easy for me to purposefully wade—dive? cannonball?!—into all those uncomfortable feelings. I don't like discord. And when we're already at odds with each other, I certainly don't like making the situation even worse. But confrontation requires that we go ahead and wade in so we can achieve the ultimate goal: healing for our relationship.

Over the years we've developed some guidelines for confrontation and disagreement that have served us well—especially so when we abide by them!

Choose the Appropriate Time and Place

I've learned it's *never* wise to broadside Craig when he's hungry, tired, cranky (that one's pretty obvious), interested in a ball game, or has just walked in the door from work. (Craig's list for me would be the same, but with one addition: when I'm in the middle of a project.) Public places that don't allow for privacy are also restricting. A major reason we chose Saturday mornings (at home) for our time to talk was because it provided the necessary privacy, block of time, and ambiance. When you're considering when to have your couple time, keep all of those factors in mind. Count on this: Eventually, you're going to need to use your talk time for confrontation!

Remember: It's Us Against the Issue, Not Me Against You

At some point in your marriage, you must come to the realization that the two of you are *not* competitors. Especially during a confrontation, you shouldn't view this battle of wills as a contest where one of you wins and the other loses. If you see conflict from that perspective, *both* of you lose! That only digs the hole deeper before you've even begun to attempt fixing what's broken.

Instead, you need to grasp that since God made you one flesh, you now have the perspective that anything that threatens your bond is the "opponent." *That* person or issue is the foe that *both* of you must battle. During conflict, rather than viewing yourselves as being on opposite teams, intent upon winning, proving *I am right,* you must cling to a totally different perspective: We are both on the same team. Together, we will fight *for* us and *against* the issue that threatens our union.

• •

Can you grasp the magnitude of the difference of "us against the issue" versus "me against you"? How can you move to this approach in your marriage? What must you change in order to gain this new perspective?

• •

Do you like being on the winning team? A gentle reminder during your next confrontation may help both of you operate from this vantage point, even during the most intense moments. Once you've worked through those issues, you'll know your team has just won!

Give Careful Attention to the Approach

We've all heard the saying that you needn't use a hammer on another's head to get his or her attention. (Except possibly a mule. Or a teenager.) Yet in symbolic terms, we've all done that at least once when confronting a spouse. Is it because our emotions are so intense? We think we must make our point immediately? Or because we're frantic to rectify the situation? Whatever the reason, by hammering on our spouses—landing "blows" that only put them into defensive mode—we've hindered, slowed, and potentially stopped the restoration process.

Instead, we need to use great skill, as Merry does when confronting her husband: "I know I need to prepare what I say to Gerald because I can cause hurt and tear down his self-esteem. I need to think about what I say, how I say it, use a 'little sugar' if the topic is hard to swallow. Words once said cannot be retrieved!"

Within Merry's wisdom are three key points: First, we need to prepare beforehand what we'll say and how we'll say it. If you're postponing confrontation until your scheduled talk time, then you certainly have no excuse for not planning ahead and choosing appropriate words, contexts, analogies, even tone of voice.

••

Can you think of a time when advance preparation would have bene-fited a confrontation? What "sugar" could you have applied to the situation?

••

Second, Merry also notes that a "little sugar" will soften the blow. For example, maybe you need to point out one of your mate's character traits that, in public, is damaging to your self-esteem. Try phrasing it this way: "Sweetheart, you are excellent at telling funny stories. Everyone—including me!—eagerly lines up when you begin a monologue. But when that story is about *me,* would you please ask my permission first?"

Third, Merry's advice is absolutely true: Spoken words cannot be retrieved. Planning beforehand and carefully choosing some words— and discarding others—will hopefully keep you from intense regret.

Agree to Avoid Name-Calling

In our first year of marriage we discovered this necessity to never, under any circumstances, call each other a name during an argument. The original cause of our disagreement, the details of the actual confrontation, and even the emotions would dissipate long before those hurtful names were forgotten. If the goal of your confrontation is to identify hurt feelings and heal them, why add more fuel to the fire? Clinging like a horrible nightmare, those unkind words cannot be taken back. Unwarranted accusations such as "only an idiot would think that way!" assault the *person* rather than the *behavior.*

• •

Have you ever called each other names? Share how wounding that is. What can you do to find the resolve to stop this habit?

• •

Once we decided that name-calling was too painful to continue, the habit had already been formed. So it took us some time to stop, consider the pain that would be inflicted on the other, and learn enough discipline to control the outbursts. Key to changing our behavior was an honest and intense discussion about how deeply those names wounded. With that sharing fresh in our memories, we soon learned the discipline to better control our tongues.

Recognize the Powerful Role of Emotions

Years ago Craig was quick to dismiss the importance and validity of emotions. He argued that feelings should be mistrusted; instead, he pronounced that logic and rational decisions were controllable and therefore superior. He now admits that he was terrified of his own emotions. The fact that feelings cannot be governed (note again that we're defining a feeling as the *instant* core emotion that originates from your heart) made him feel insecure and out of control. For that reason, Craig would either submerge or deny their existence in his life. For years he was able to do that—for himself. But denying *my* emotions? That was another matter entirely! Mine were rather tough to ignore when they had been ignited by conflict!

The need to recognize the power of emotions would have many ramifications for our relationship. One of the most significant was in the area of control. Remember in the previous chapter when we talked about *controlling an argument* versus *controlling me*? In the past, Craig's skill in debating determined who managed our arguments: He controlled the agenda, the direction, the outcome. Even the tone of his voice and implications ("How could any sane, rational person disagree with me?") could so intimidate that I would either respond with great defensiveness or merely shut down.

But the main areas of control—those related to my feelings—were even more subtle. When I would express emotions (and admittedly, probably with exuberance), Craig would attempt to control the argument—control me—by dismissing the feelings. "You shouldn't feel that way" or "Why would you feel that way?" or "That's an overreaction!" are not acceptable responses simply because *I don't need to justify my feelings.* One caution, however: Make sure that you are expressing a feeling and not a judgment. If you can substitute the phrases "I think that" or "I judge that" before expressing a feeling, then you have *not* expressed an emotion. (Compare "I feel that you need to apologize" as opposed to "I feel crushed; I judge that you need to apologize.")

• •

Do you ask each other to "justify" feelings in any way? How? How has this impeded your intimacy? Can you think of an issue in which you need to apply these principles of revealing each other's angry or painful feelings in an atmosphere of acceptance?

• •

To keep an argument from being controlled by your spouse, you must keep coming back to that simple—and yet incredibly difficult—concept: *Emotions just are. I have the right to express them. This is not a judgment of your behavior or character—it's just me.* How does one argue with that? An important part of this learned skill is digging out the feelings beneath the feelings, because that process will eventually get you to the ultimate goal: finding the core issue and healing your relationship.

Remember also that emotions don't exist in a vacuum. Underneath anger may reside rejection, fear, depression, or woundedness. When your spouse is attempting to control your argument, these are the types of heartfelt expressions you need to share: "But hear me—I felt attacked when that happened. I may have initially responded with anger, but I felt heartbroken and experienced a knifelike pain. I still feel broken, as though my spirit has been crushed. And now I feel worthless and isolated and alone." Rather than provoke your spouse toward defensive responses, those words will direct you in a positive way toward reconciliation.

Granted, the skill of effectively sharing emotions takes continual practice. Craig and I didn't acquire this technique in a month or in a year. Truthfully, we're still learning how to do this well. But the consistent determination to accept each other's feelings (and therefore, each other) would point us toward the ultimate goal of our confrontation: getting to the core of the problem. For, as stated in chapter 3, our emotions reveal met or unmet needs. And somewhere, buried under layers of hurt and anger, protected by defensiveness and barriers, lies the core of the problem: an unmet need.

Cut to the Core Issues

During confrontation, sharing feelings is not the ultimate goal; finding the heart of the problem between us is. However, remember that emotions function as red- or green-light indicators. That's how we *use* emotions to get to the heart of the issue, to direct us toward those unmet needs. Emotions are incredible tools. Our job is to learn how to use them effectively.

In our marriage, the simple matter of getting ready for a meeting or social engagement was prime territory for conflict. It seemed we were always late leaving the house. On one particular occasion several years ago, I (Craig) don't remember where we were supposed to be or why. But I do clearly recall that Carolyn was the reason we were late, so I was extremely angry. At her. And I let her know it, biting at her in an outburst of cutting words. I also remember that she reacted with obvious hurt. Instantly recoiling from me with pronounced pain on her face, she then physically moved away from me in the car. It was going to be a long evening.

Don't you hate it when you have to "fake it" in public situations? I'm sure we smiled, greeted people, acted as though all was right in our world. But inside, both of us were miserable. Carolyn made definite attempts to *not* touch me all evening—when normally we would naturally and easily lean against each other or hold hands. No one else probably noticed, but there was a barrier between us that felt tangible, physically and emotionally.

By the time we got home, we were exhausted from our churning emotions and the monumental effort to hide them. Though tempted to simply fall into bed, I knew Carolyn was too hurt for us to put this off a moment longer. And besides, I was miserable too. The million-dollar question: What precipitated my incredible outburst of anger? Why was I so obsessed with being on time?

As always, it took a while to get past our initial feelings of anger and hurt. The emotion in the room was so intense that Carolyn resisted opening up at first. Then our defensiveness came to the fore: She accused me of not merely desiring to be on time, but ridiculously early. I had to admit that was true, but I immediately shot back that she knew this was important to me. Carolyn argued that it couldn't be helped because of last-minute delays that weren't her fault. All that was peripheral to the issue, however, and we knew it. Eventually, we started digging into my anger to discover what was beneath it. And there I discovered panic, an anxiety that led me to be obsessed about not only being on time but early. Finally, a memory from childhood surfaced.

I was in elementary school, probably about ten years of age. At that time, my dad was drinking heavily, and Mom was barely coping with the stress of living with an alcoholic. I can remember being elated that I'd made the final cut for the baseball team, and how emphatic the coach was about our being at the ball field early to warm up before the game. "Either be there for practice—*or you don't play.* Simple as that!" he'd drilled over and over. I remember thinking to myself, *No way I'm gonna be late. I'm playing!*

However, it was game day, and neither of my folks could take me to the field. I had no friends nearby to give me a ride. I had only one option: the bus. After the frantic process of finding the right line, making the necessary changes, and finally heading in the right direction, I glanced at my watch and realized with a sinking dread that there was no possibility I'd be on time for warmups. So I sat there, watching every miserable minute pass by. Stewing, sweating, heart racing, knowing that my fate was sealed. When I finally arrived at the field, I was soundly chewed out by the coach in front of the entire team. And I did indeed sit the bench that day. The hurt from that single incident would leave an everlasting impression on me: I determined I would never be late again.

I (Carolyn) still feel pain, and my eyes fill with tears when I picture the little boy on that bus. I can see him so clearly: dressed in his baseball uniform, antsy, frantic, despairing. Surrounded by people, he was still all alone. He was forced into a situation that no child of that age should ever face—responsibility way beyond his years, consequences he didn't deserve, trauma that would never completely leave his life. I longed to cradle him in my arms. Maybe since I'm the mother of two sons, the image is just too real. And too tender.

When Craig shared that story, my hurt and anger instantly melted away, for I saw him in a totally new light. I could feel his desperation and despair, and they became mine too. As feelings of tenderness moved from the child to the man before me, I realized that though he was now a grown man, all the emotions of the child were *still there.* And from that moment on, I would view his need to be on time through the picture of that desperate little boy on a bus.

Not every confrontation ends with the discovery of a past painful experience. But disciplined and focused detective work should lead you to discover some facet of an unmet need that has caused the initial problem. In this situation, we found that Craig's need for autonomy had taken a direct hit when he was late for ball practice as a boy. It's intensely important for him to be seen as a person who takes responsibility for himself and gets the job done. Feeling all that slip away on that bus left him with a void he would attempt to fill from then on—by never being late again.

••

Review and discuss the four basic needs: love, belonging, self-worth, and autonomy. How are these being fulfilled—or not fulfilled—in your life? How can you be more attuned to these in the future when you'll need to "cut to the core problem"?

••

Cutting to the core of an issue will always be a challenge predicated on the truth that our natural defenses put up barriers to vulnerability. In chapter 5, we listed the four basic needs and questions to direct and aid your discovery work. If necessary, review those to work on a specific issue in your marriage.

Seek Solutions That Bring Restoration

Craig and I had solved the mystery of why he was so intent upon being on time. Our in-depth, intimate communication removed the intense feelings, and I gained a great sensitivity to Craig's needs in this area, making it a priority to attempt to leave the house on time. However, note my emphasis upon the word *attempt*. I wish I could say that I was never late again, but my good intentions still sometimes fail as I equate *being on time* with "only five minutes late." Craig views it as "ten minutes early." You don't need a calculator to discover a fifteen-minute gap for Craig's pacing while I rush! While I continue to work hard at being on time, I think that Craig has put into place his own devious plan: I'm convinced that he's set every clock in the house at least five minutes early!

Other issues are obviously of a more serious nature, and these call for major commitments and promises to change. When one spouse has been deeply wounded by the other, both need to work through those intense feelings. Chapter 12 will give even more suggestions about how to make sure you share those in a way that allows healing to take place. But right on the heels of processing emotions is the reality that the offending spouse must follow up those words with action: He or she needs to *change*. Listening, accepting, and embracing your spouse's hurt feelings; asking forgiveness; and promises of repentance mean little if the offending spouse continues to be a workaholic who grants only crumbs of time to the relationship, lies, or belittles his or her mate.

Not all conflict, however, involves intense experiences from the past, layers of emotions to work through, or a prolonged process for healing to take place. Instead, you may simply need to agree to changes such as Gerald and Merry share. When Gerald repeatedly kept "losing his temper and patience with drivers who don't abide by the driving laws," they decided upon a creative solution. Merry says she suggested to her husband that "instead of yelling, blood pressure rising, and letting it ruin his day, he sing 'Jesus Loves Me.'" She continues: "This simple act has brought him patience, laughter, enjoyment! We now laugh about these incidences when he shares that he had to sing that day. Since I also sing 'Jesus Loves Me' when I'm confronted with negative thoughts, we'll call each other and ask, 'Have you had to sing today?' This usually brings a hearty laugh at the beginning of the conversation!"

....

In what areas do you need to seek solutions? Can you "think outside the lines" like Merry, suggesting ideas that infuse fun? Are there other issues between you of a more serious nature? Where have you stalled in the process of finding healing—in discovering the core issue, processing emotions, granting and receiving forgiveness, or committing to real change?

....

The Aftermath: Seeking Forgiveness

When one of us has deeply hurt the other, we dare not attempt to rush the process of forgiving. Yes, it's a *process.* Scripture is quite clear that we are to forgive: "Forgive as the Lord forgave you" (Colossians 3:13) is not a mere suggestion. However, because our emotions are indelibly tied to forgiving, we must separate the two parts of the process. Maybe most important of all—understand and accept that there *are* two distinct parts.

1. The Initial Jump

First order of need: a true apology. A quickly muttered, superficial "I'm sorry" is not sufficient. The offending spouse needs to look the other directly in the eyes and ask, "Will you forgive me?" That calls for the offender to truly humble himself/herself before the other; of equal import is that the one offended must also *decide*—and *respond.* Both question and answer call for action, because forgiveness is about doing.

2. Continued Healing

Emotions are stubborn. They don't care to be packaged, beaten into submission, or submerged for a great amount of time. And they certainly won't be rushed. Like a grocery cart with wobbly wheels, they'll fight your efforts to hurry them before they're finished, extinguished, and healed.

We once heard a speaker say that "a woman can't really forgive her husband until he can describe to her how she feels." We agree, except that we judge that may be equally true for the hurting husband. Therefore, this part of the healing process also calls for work, patience, and diligence by the wounded partner *and* the offender. The spouse who's been hurt must lovingly describe those feelings; the offender then attempts to relate those emotions in his or her own words. ("Did you feel like…?" or "I think I felt that same way when I experienced…")

Even if you both handle this part of the process with great sensitivity and care, those hurt feelings may linger. The deeper the wound, the longer the healing process takes. Therefore, both spouses must give each other a gift: The wounded spouse acts as though the forgiveness process is *done,* to the best of his or her ability. At the same time, the offender grants the other spouse the time he or she needs to completely heal. We'll discuss how to do this in greater detail in the next chapter.

Some wounds are so deep that you may benefit from professional counseling. Please don't hesitate to seek that help if you find that you cannot process this on your own. We also highly recommend Lewis Smedes's book *The Art of Forgiving* for additional help in this area.

In Love and Prayer

You may not realize this, but confronting takes an incredible amount of love—love for the person you're confronting. Only one who loves another deeply will put the relationship at risk by pointing out "This is a flaw I see in you," or "You have hurt me in this way." That person cares enough about the other to also put his own emotions at risk.

John and Laura lovingly demonstrate this when they say, "We

hesitantly confess to one another and point out, hopefully gently and in a loving spirit, each other's faults. We don't just point out preferences for how we want the other person to be, but truth, like, 'You are wrong in this, and if you weren't so angry, you could see this.'" *That's* love—demonstrated in courageous action.

••

Does one of you need to forgive the other? Or do you need to ask for forgiveness? Where are you in the process of sharing, discovering the core issues, and healing? If you have granted forgiveness, have your feelings caught up to your words?

••

Finally, we cannot emphasize strongly enough the healing power of praying together. We can't explain that miraculous healing. And maybe it's not meant to be explained. But when a couple is in conflict, sincere prayer has the ability to provide a secure red rope to safety like Rahab's cord. Dwayne and Pam's touching words bear repeating: "At times of crisis, praying together has literally held us together."

don't attempt to fix me; just listen to my heart!

How Do Our Emotions Impact Forgiveness?

raig is an excellent problem solver with the ability to discern the core issue that has broken a relationship, zero in, and then list off the solutions, all in about sixty seconds. Say it, sort it, solve it. *Next?* Meanwhile, I'm still back at stage one. My feelings are still forming, evolving, and making themselves known. I may not even know precisely what I'm feeling at this point, let alone be able to share all that with Craig! But he has already moved on, convinced that we're ready to put this baby to rest. That's when my heart cries, *Now, just hold on a moment, will you?*

Once Craig and I finally settled the issue that feelings do have relevance and significance, we still needed to learn the importance of adequate processing time. How I wish my emotions would give me a clear timetable, printing a readout something like this: *The praise from your supervisor was deserved, and your feelings of optimism and enthusiasm are a driving force in all areas of your life. Count on that continuing for a week.* Or how about, *You've been ridiculed, and now you feel embarrassed and insecure. It will take two months to leave those feelings in the dust.* Armed with those facts, I could plan the following days accordingly. I could inform Craig, "Rough road ahead. It's gonna take two full weeks for me to get over that." I can't imagine the grief that kind of knowledge would spare Craig *and* me! Unfortunately, I have no idea how long those feelings—both the red- and green-light emotions—will be a companion to my days. The emotions take the reins and I hang on for the ride!

In light of that, how do we handle an open-ended timetable for processing our emotions? Here are some suggestions to get you through the waiting period.

BEGIN BY MERELY SHARING EMOTIONS

The first stage of the waiting period begins when you start sharing your emotions with each other. You both need to accept the legitimacy of this stage. I (Carolyn) love cake. Let me correct that: I love *icing* (buttercream, to be precise). So I eat cake mostly to enjoy the payoff—the icing. However, I'm not implying that I merely endure the cake; instead, I judge that cake highlights and enhances the taste of icing, making it significantly more enjoyable than eating icing alone (although that option has pluses too). Processing emotions, eliminating the barriers between us, and solving the issues are quite similar to my appreciation for cake: We definitely need the cake (giving our emotions the time they need to heal) to enjoy the icing (resolving the issues).

•••

Do you agree that sharing feelings is an essential part of the healing process? Which one of you may take longer at this than the other? How can both of you demonstrate appreciation and patience for this need?

•••

When Craig and I first learned this technique, we were both guilty of being impatient with the timing of the process. I'd share my emotions,

Craig would succinctly validate them, and then we assumed we were ready to move on to problem solving. Maybe a day or so later, I'd note the same feelings resurfacing. At that point, Craig would be angry that these emotions were still hanging around, while I'd feel defensive and disgusted at myself (on top of the original feelings, of course!). What we hadn't yet learned was that we needed to allow those feelings to be fully expressed—without any pressure to move to problem solving, period.

We began to understand that sharing feelings was not something to be endured and quickly moved through. Instead, it was a valid and integral part of our problem-solving process. When we both fully accepted that, we gave our feelings the time and attention they needed. I didn't rush my sharing or feel guilty for taking so long. And Craig granted me the time I needed, understanding that I take longer at this than he does.

THE SPOUSE SHARING HIS OR HER HEART SETS THE TIMETABLE

When Carolyn was expecting our first child, we attended childbirth classes, learning the breathing and timing techniques to make delivery as smooth as possible. We attended the classes faithfully and practiced diligently. I'm telling you, we had those techniques *mastered.* So when Carolyn entered the final stage of labor and contractions were very severe, I was even more determined to make sure we did this right, stayed on schedule, and did everything according to plan. I was timing a contraction on my watch's second hand to an exact sixty seconds, instructing Carolyn to *stop* the breathing technique at that moment. But she shot me a furious glare and hissed through clenched teeth, *"It's not over yet!"* Right then I should've learned this simple principle: The one in pain sets the timetable!

I (Craig) can work through my feelings pretty quickly. Discovering and uncovering my emotions has become easier through the years, and now I find that they're nearer the surface than they've ever been—much more so than I'm comfortable with, to be truthful! Once I verbalize them, giving them names and brief descriptions, I'm pretty much ready to move on. Speaking those feelings out loud seems to take away their power instantly, and I find release in that exercise.

··

Can you think of a time when one of you was hurting and the other tried to rush the healing process? Do you need to come back to that situation now for healing in your relationship? What can you do to ensure that you give each other all the time that each of you requires?

··

Carolyn, however, needs just a tad more time. She'll express her emotions. Repackage them. Describe them. Say them again. Vent. Yell. Cry. And maybe *then* be ready to move on! If I sound as though I'm ridiculing her, I'm truly not. For I've discovered that her emotions run deep. Allowing her to fully dig those out and express them takes not only time but an appreciation on my part for the hard work this is for her—and the gift that she's giving to me by trusting me with her innermost feelings.

Most important, I've learned to never say, "Now here are some solutions" until Carolyn clearly indicates that we're ready to move on to that step. She alone decides when that's appropriate—just as I decide when I'm ready to move on. If I attempt to rush the process, negate her needs by insisting that "it's time to move on," or exhibit impatience, then I've only hindered our progress. Don't shortchange either step, or you'll only find yourselves circling back anyway!

SOMETIMES THERE IS ONLY ONE STAGE

I (Craig) do enjoy solving problems. Wired to drive to the core issue, apply the needed solution, and wrap up one more project, I tend to desire the same outcome with my wife. However, after years of attempting to do just that, I finally got this clear message from Carolyn: "Sometimes I don't want to be fixed. And I don't want answers. I just want you to listen to my heart." I fought it, still don't fully understand it, and maybe still feel uneasy when Carolyn asks me to just...*listen.* But I have come to accept that sometimes her soul needs to do exactly that— simply share her deepest emotions with me in an atmosphere of unconditional love and acceptance. And nothing more.

••

Do either of you have a need to be listened to in this way: to share your deepest emotions freely, in an atmosphere of unconditional love and acceptance? How can your spouse help to encourage this? Can you think of a topic to use in practicing these skills?

••

To facilitate this, we've agreed to take away any possible misunderstandings and miscommunication by Carolyn's directly stating, "Sweetheart, this is one of those times. Just listen to my heart." Eventually, even bullheaded fixers like me get *that* message!

FORGIVENESS IS A TWO-STEP PROCESS

In the previous chapter on confrontation, we discussed the fact that forgiveness has two definite steps: the act of *deciding* to forgive and then the *healing* of wounded emotions. The first step, the decision, is an instant mandate. By an act of our will, we decide to grant forgiveness. However, experiencing fully healed emotions involves a process that may take days, weeks, months, years. And rather than trying to force the healing of emotions by an act of our will, we must wait for the feelings to ease at their own pace. Each part of this process is a delicate balancing act; if either part gets out of balance, then both you and your marriage suffer. Therefore, we need to discuss these two steps and their ramifications in greater detail.

When the offended spouse says, "I forgive you," he or she has agreed to operate *as though the entire two-step process is complete.* That means that he or she will *attempt to not...*

- intentionally withhold love—emotionally or physically.
- punish the offender.
- seek revenge or retribution.
- erect barriers to intimacy.

In many ways, forgiving a spouse parallels the forgiveness we receive from a righteous God: He sees us as fully righteous the moment we are saved (because he views us through his Son), despite the fact that we're still sinful children.

But here's the paradox: The offender must grant the wounded spouse *all the time he or she needs to reach complete healing.* This means that the offender will *attempt to not...*

- demand love—emotionally or physically.
- respond defensively or negatively to a spouse's pain, wariness, or insecurity.
- seek instant acceptance.
- expect immediate intimacy.

• •

Can you think of a time when you wish you had applied this paradox for healing? Do you agree with those goals listed previously? Discuss practical examples of how these goals might work out in your marriage.

• •

Many have symbolically compared being deeply wounded by another to a burn: Even after the burned area heals, the skin will remain sensitive for some time—possibly forever, depending on the severity of the burn. Therefore, if the offended person has been seriously hurt, he or she will need the offender to be patient, considerate, and gracious throughout the time of healing. And although the offended one sets the timetable for healing, he or she should make a strong effort to work toward healing.

Let Go of Martyrdom

Whenever I've been hurt by something Craig has said or done, my first instinct is always the same: Wrapping my pain around me like a banner, I withdraw to a stronghold of martyrdom. There I hide, protecting myself from further hurt *and* preventing a resolution. In a self-absorbed way, I *want* to be alone there; I seem to desire wallowing in that pain for a while. More important, I admit to wanting Craig to also feel alone and miserable. "After all, he deserves to feel hurt too!" I tell myself.

> Can either of you recall a time when you were a "false martyr"? Did that help your relationship—or damage it? Can you grasp the difference between a legitimate time to heal and clinging to your pain? How can you hold each other accountable for maintaining a balance between the decision to forgive and the time needed to heal broken emotions?

However, that type of martyrdom is entirely self-inflicted—a false imitation of the real thing. With motivations that are entirely selfish and self-destructive, I not only make myself miserable, but I certainly don't help our relationship either. While raising a "righteous banner" of hurt, I'm not acting righteously at all. Instead, I'm intentionally saying no to working through the issues before us.

The dilemma is this: How do you determine if you're intentionally clinging to your pain or actively attempting to release it? How do you know when you're merely being a false martyr or legitimately needing more time to heal within? Only you can determine the answers through intentional, intense, and intimate prayer. If you come to God with a sincere desire to forgive your spouse, to evaluate your deepest motivations, and to heal your relationship with your spouse, then God will guide you toward what your mind, will, and heart need to do to find resolution.

Once again we point you to the Source. He awaits your intimate relationship. And he longs to help you forgive.

Ever begin a project when your intuitions were whispering that to proceed might be a mistake? Or that if you did continue, you'd best do so Indiana Jones style, watching for quicksand, ambushes, and land mines along the way? *That's* what writing this book has felt like sometimes! First of all, a close friend once looked us squarely in the eyes and warned, "Just don't *ever* write a book on marriage!" We're not sure what his biases and concerns were, but we look up to him as a godly and wise man. His was a caution that we couldn't easily dismiss.

Then we mulled over our own list of hesitations. Had we any right to address such an intangible topic as spiritual growth in marriage in the first place? Is it even describable? That impossible task feels like attempting to hold water in your hand. Then we wondered if we could write this book without appearing to position ourselves as shining examples. Also, what consequences could we potentially face for being vulnerable, exposing our lives and innermost feelings in a book? (Talk about potential land mines and quicksand!) And lastly, we both avoid—like the plague—the "Ten Easy Steps to Anything!" approach to books. We wondered if we could speak to this important process without reverting to an easy-solution formula.

Obviously we elected to proceed, but not without considerable prayer and never minus those nagging questions. Only time will tell whether we managed to avoid the quicksand and land mines!

No matter where we were in the writing process, we had to forge ahead with a consistent tension: We are *not* worthy to write a book on marriage because our relationship is far from perfect. At the same time, we determined that if you can learn and grow from our experience, if you can profit from our mistakes, then the risk was worth taking. At the same time, please know how much we feel the weight of this responsibility *before our God.* Before *you.*

Remember the story about the time I (Carolyn) got locked out of church and how painful that experience was for me? I didn't write a warm and fuzzy ending to that *because it didn't happen.* When I tried to discuss my hurt feelings with Craig, he quickly dismissed them. "You're holding a grudge!" and "Isn't this a pretty big overreaction to a silly mistake?" were his responses. Feeling guilty for my stubborn feelings that wouldn't fade, I tucked them away, carrying the hurt (martyr style—some of us are pros at that technique) for years.

We had a tremendous amount of growing to do at that point in our lives—*and we still do.* For we're on this same journey with you toward intimacy, maturity, and spiritual growth. The questions that we must continually ask ourselves are these: "Are we still working on our marriage? Are we continuing on this journey of proactive and intentional growth?"

If we have implied that we've arrived in our marriage, then hear this clearly: We've been through many rough waters. Sometimes we've handled those well; other times we haven't. We also recognize that we'll face more times of trial in the years to come. For no matter where we are in our journey, there are still numerous challenges ahead, mistakes to be made, and then, hopefully, lessons learned from those blunders. And honestly, isn't that the exciting part? That no matter where we are—newlyweds, middle age, empty nest, or retirement—we can still learn and grow together, becoming more and more a true team in the process? What a challenge!

Finally, let us state this with absolute sincerity: *We care about your marriage.* In turn, you should care about ours and also every other marriage in your sphere of influence. For every time there's discord or divorce within the body of Christ, we *all* feel the reverberating effects.

Like pulsating circles of damage from an earthquake, your pain affects us; our hurt touches you. Isn't that what being a part of the body of Christ is all about—that we're connected on a deep level because of the Holy Spirit's indwelling?

Romans 12:5 describes this concept in an awe-inspiring way when it states, "So in Christ we who are many form one body, and each member *belongs* to all the others" (emphasis added). If we are to take that to heart—and certainly we should—then we'd best be about caring, nurturing, investing in, and being responsible for one another. To the point that we accept the truth that we *belong* to others in the body. What a life-changing concept that could be for us all if we were to actually live that out in our marriages and in the community of believers.

In the introduction, we talked about our guarantee to you: We challenged you to try this method of communicating with intent and intensity, and if you weren't satisfied with the results, you could have your old relationship back. So now, the phrase of "put up or shut up!" comes to mind. It's time to make those choices. What risks will *you* take? Will you work hard to attempt change? Or will you be satisfied with a status quo marriage? Which relationship do you desire—the old, safe, unchanging one or a new relationship that will be forged out of love, courage, intent, and intensity?

As for us, we need to run. Saturday morning and two great mugs of coffee are waiting.

To learn more about WaterBrook Press and view
our catalog of products, log on to our Web site:
www.waterbrookpress.com

WATERBROOK
PRESS